Horace Seaver

Occasional thoughts of Horace Seaver

From fifty years of free thinking

Horace Seaver

Occasional thoughts of Horace Seaver
From fifty years of free thinking

ISBN/EAN: 9783337277796

Printed in Europe, USA, Canada, Australia, Japan

Cover: Foto ©Suzi / pixelio.de

More available books at **www.hansebooks.com**

OCCASIONAL THOUGHTS

OF

HORACE SEAVER,

FROM

FIFTY YEARS OF FREE THINKING.

SELECTED FROM
The Boston Investigator.

"Come forth into the light of things,
Let Nature be your Teacher."
Wordsworth.

BOSTON:
PUBLISHED BY J. P. MENDUM,
Investigator Office,
PAINE MEMORIAL BUILDING,
APPLETON STREET.
1888.

PREFACE.

THIS volume is made up of editorials written for the *Investigator* by Mr Seaver. It has been prepared with his knowledge and consent, but without consulting his judgment as to its contents.

The responsibility of selecting the articles for this book was assumed without thought of criticism. The desire which prompted the work, and directed its preparation, was to preserve, in a more convenient form, the writings of one who has honored the cause of free thought by his ability and devotion, and who is honored and respected, by thousands of his fellow beings, as the Nestor of Liberalism.

No apology need be offered for giving this book to the world. It carries its own recommendation. Every friend of honest thought will welcome it as a valuable addition to the library of honest literature, which is yet none too large. Every father who is desirous of having a wise instructor for the growing minds of his children will be glad to take this volume into his home.

A new generation, which is to carry forward the work of emancipation from the bondage of superstition, is coming upon the stage of action. The counsel of the generation which is now passing away should be heeded. No man of his time has spoken wiser words than Horace Seaver.

If the lessons contained in this volume could be transmuted into human character and human life, the individual would be nobler, society would be purer, and the nation would be better.

Let us remember that it is not only wisdom to speak wise words, but also to heed them.

L. K. WASHBURN.

REVERE, Mass, Aug. 24, 1888.

CONTENTS.

	PAGE
OPPOSITION AND PREJUDICE	9
EDUCATION A CURE FOR BIGOTRY	11
CIRCUMSTANCES	13
GOVERNMENT	14
WOMAN'S RIGHTS	17
SOCIETY	20
THE SCHOOLMASTER	21
PRIESTS	22
FREE DISCUSSION	23
THE TRIUMPH OF LEARNING	24
HINTS TO HERETICS	25
THE THEATRE	26
WHO IS THE ATHEIST?	28
TEMPERANCE	30
INDIVIDUAL EFFORT	32
HEAVEN AND HELL	33
RELIGIOUS DESPOTISMS	34
CONSCIENCE	35
TO ADVOCATE UNWELCOME TRUTHS NO EASY TASK	36
AGITATION	37
OPINIONS	38
EXAGGERATION	39
THE QUESTION	40
THE PRESENT AGE	41
THOMAS PAINE	43
SELF-RESPECT	44
SECTARIANISM	45
THE WORKING-CLASS	47
REFORMERS	49
LIBERTY	51

CONTENTS.

MOTIVES	52
VIRTUE AND RELIGION	53
BAD INTENTIONS	54
"THE WORLD MOVES"	55
RELIGION AND LIBERALISM	56
SUNDAY SCHOOLS	59
REVERENCE FOR OLD DOCTRINES	61
COURAGE	63
FREE SPEECH	64
THE CLOSING YEAR	65
THE UNKNOWN	67
WHAT WILL YOU SUBSTITUTE FOR RELIGION?	68
INDIVIDUALITY	70
FREEDOM OF THE PRESS	74
DIFFERENCE OF OPINION	76
REFLECTIONS	77
MOTHERS	79
PHILOSOPHY AND RELIGION	81
LIFE A JOURNEY	82
THE GREAT PURPOSE OF SOCIAL LIFE	83
NATURE AND REASON	85
PURPOSES OF LIFE	86
PUNISHMENT	87
RIGHT DOCTRINE	89
LEARNING A TRADE	89
HOME CONVERSATION	91
IMPROVEMENT OF MANKIND	93
THIS WORLD	96
A FUTURE LIFE	97
THE INFLUENCE OF WOMAN	98
OLD AGE	101
LIGHT AND DARKNESS	102
PRIDE	106
LIVING AND DYING	108
INTELLECTUAL PLEASURES	109
EVILS	113
DUTY AND HAPPINESS	114
UNIVERSAL BENEVOLENCE	115
TRUTH	117

CONTENTS.

PLEASURES	121
LIBERTY — REASON — JUSTICE — SOCIETY	124
IMAGINATION	127
LITERATURE — EDUCATION — JUSTICE	131
WORDS — IDEAS	133
MAKE THE BEST OF EVERYTHING	137
INTELLECTUAL IMPROVEMENT	139
ACTIONS — DUTIES — VIRTUES	140
MOTHERS AND CHILDREN	144
AMUSEMENTS ON SUNDAY	148
THE TRAINING OF CHILDREN	151
PHYSICAL EDUCATION	152
REFORM	154
THOUGHTS FOR THE YOUNG	155
THE RIGHT TO EXPRESS OPINIONS	158
PREACHING	161
THE SUPPLY OF NATURAL WANTS	164
THE RIGHT TO GOOD GOVERNMENT	168
FEMALE INFLUENCE	171
IMPORTANCE OF COMMON SCHOOLS	173
THE CLERGY AND REFORM	175
VIRTUE AND VICE	177
PROVIDENCE	180
EDITING	182
A CHEERFUL PHILOSOPHY	183
A NOBLE LIFE	185
ACTIONS	186
RIGHTS	187
RELIGION AND COMMON SENSE	188
SCIENCE AND RELIGION	190
THOUGHTS ON LIFE AND DEATH	194
FOLLOW THE LIGHT OF EVIDENCE	198
WHAT IS TRUTH?	202
MAN	205
WHAT HUMANITY NEEDS	208
SECTARIAN SCHOOLS	210
INDIVIDUALITY	212
SUNDAY	213
INFIDELITY	215

CONTENTS.

THE INTELLECTUAL FACULTIES	216
FREEDOM OF OPINION	217
PROTESTANTS — CATHOLICS	219
MORAL INFLUENCE	220
RELIGION IN THE PUBLIC SCHOOLS	221
FORMATION OF OPINIONS	222
A CHURCH	223
BLIND FAITH	224
IGNORANCE AND DEVOTION	225
CRIME	227
MORALITY	228
THIS WORLD	229

OCCASIONAL THOUGHTS.

OPPOSITION AND PREJUDICE.

It would be difficult to find, in the general prejudice against the advocates of our principles, any justifiable motive for that prejudice. We are not to be understood to assert that there are none who honestly and conscientiously oppose us. We have no doubt there are many. But this is no proof that their opposition is founded on correct grounds, and is therefore right and expedient. Man may be as conscientious in error, as in truth, but it is error, nevertheless; and the opposition it creates, however sincere, is none the less unjust.

While, then, we admit that we have some conscientious opposers, we are no less conscientious in affirming that their opposition and prejudice are based on error; and consequently their conduct cannot be justified. That this is the truth, is apparent from our doctrine itself; for it contains nothing that any man in his right senses can honestly reject. We profess to believe only in things known and seen,—things that have been demonstrated by actual observation or experience, and of course known to be what they are represented. This we call knowledge; and the only knowledge in the world worthy of the name. Who can advance a valid or reasonable objection to this belief? We disbelieve, on the other hand, only what is unseen and unknown, and cannot be seen or known. But here is no disbelief of knowledge involved. And who, we ask again, can rationally object to this belief?

These two principles comprise, in substance, the doctrine for which we contend. And, we repeat, it is difficult on any reasonable and honest ground to account for the bitter opposition it has drawn down upon those who support it.

They who conscientiously oppose our doctrine, have doubtless never examined the foundation on which it rests; but, taking counsel from others, have formed a judgment from the representations of persons interested in deceiving them. Honest themselves, they have given implicit credence to what they deemed the honesty of others; without any examination, on their own part, of the truth of the charges preferred against us. But the great majority of our opposers are sheer calumniators, who, in order to fix upon us the detestation of the public, and to secure the safety of their "craft," brand us with opprobrious epithets which excite the prejudice and animosity of the people, and suppress the spirit of inquiry, the exercise of which would enable them to judge for themselves.

Let us, however, continue to persevere in the cause we have embraced, and make our examples prove the truth of our principles. So shall Free Inquiry eventually prevail over all opposition,

EDUCATION A CURE FOR BIGOTRY.

Ignorance is not only the mother of superstition, she is also the parent of fear. He who has no definite knowledge of what he professes to believe, is not only afraid openly to avow his sentiments, and firmly to maintain them, but he is also afraid to have them very closely examined. The consequence is, that if he possesses any power over those that are about him, he finds it far easier to propagate and defend his opinions by the awe of his authority, than by the clearness of his explanations and the force of his arguments. Hence, an ignorant people are afraid of frank inquiry and close investigation, not so much, perhaps, because they fear the skepticism of others, as because they dread the exposure of their own ignorance.

It is here, then, that bigotry begins to fetter the powers of the human mind, and to chain it in a thraldom far more distressing than the imprisonment of the body. Among an ignorant people, the child is not permitted, with freedom, to express its sentiments. To dare to doubt what has been said to be true by its friends and its relations, is to subject itself, if not to their censure, at least to their gloomy frowns and their dark suspicions. The result is, not the inculcation of correct sentiments, but the growth of an ignorant bigotry; and then, when the mind, unshackled from these early religious restraints, begins to examine for itself, there are ten thousand obstacles in the path of truth; there is still this long-cherished fear of offending those whom they have been taught to reverence and to love; there is connected with this, perhaps, a deep sense of shame, because they know so little of things with which they ought to have been familiar; there is a feeling of discouragement at the contemplation of those who are apparently firm in their convictions, and who are enjoying all the pleasures of unwavering faith; and then there is the cutting, withering conviction that they are unsettled in their opinions, and yet cannot express a doubt, without sacrificing character. It takes a firm and decided mind, particularly if one possesses warm and ardent affections, to bear up with perseverance, under the pressure of circumstances like these. And we have often thought that many an individual thus educated, or rather thus permitted to grow up in ignorance, has, in the madness of disappointed enthusiasm, rejected the truth, through fear of subjection to the bigotry of error.

Education prevents such catastrophes. It scatters light upon what is dark, instead of enveloping it in tenfold darkness. It encourages inquiry because it loves the truth. The parent who is instructed wishes the child to ask, that it may receive its instruction. Its reasonable doubts are heard with attention, and answered with candor; and the village where such a state of society exists, is a village from which bigotry flies, and in which truth makes her dwelling.

CIRCUMSTANCES.

In respect to character, man has a capacity to be anything, and by turns everything, as circumstances shall determine. He, like the floating bubble on the stream, shows us, at times, many colors and mixtures of colors; but these various shades of character, however light or dark, are little more than reflex radiations from surrounding objects and occurrences. The simple nature of man is colorless — it is fitted to receive every variety of impression; and when the combined nature and impression call forth an action, good or bad, such action discloses not so much the hue of the nature itself, as the hue which it has taken from the bright or gloomy influences to which it has been exposed.

If, therefore, we would have the family of man to be, as it were, a bright and glorious assemblage of the pictures of humanity, we must place all men in favorable positions, and surround them with circumstances and influences in which there is nothing black or unseemly. It matters not so much what may be the mere knowledge given to men, or the religious or the moral precepts taught to them, if the circumstances by which they are surrounded be disregarded;—bad circumstances and influences can neither produce nor yet maintain good men. Circumstances furnish the seed of good or ill, and man is but the soil in which they grow. The characters of men may be made entirely good or entirely bad, or, as now, a variegated mixture of good and bad; but if the institutional circumstances and influences which surround man do not accord with the end desired—do not contain within them more of good than of evil—that which was intended to be a beautiful garden will become either choked up with noxious weeds, or turned into a blighted and barren waste.

GOVERNMENT.

All the forms of government at present existing, are in a greater or less degree tyrannical and irresponsible. The wrongs which emanate from them operate upon the people, generally, in an indirect manner, through the medium of laws; and such laws are always necessarily imbued with the spirit of inequality which pervades the government from which they spring.

Might and right have long been, with rulers,

synonymous terms; and right and wisdom and virtue are supposed to be inherent in certain persons and classes of the community, independent of other persons and classes. But all these ideas of superior and inferior — of master and man — may be traced to the neglect of First Principles, and to the consequent rise of inequality of possessions; and such ideas will never be eradicated, nor the institutions founded upon them be subverted, so long as this inequality is maintained.

Men have hitherto blindly hoped to remedy the present unnatural state of things, and to institute equality of rights and laws, by removing one rich tyrant and setting up another — by destroying *existing inequality* and leaving untouched the *cause* of the inequality; but it will shortly be seen that it is not in the nature of any mere governmental change to afford permanent relief — that misgovernment is not a cause, but a consequence, — that it is not the creator, but the created, *that it is the offspring of inequality of possessions;* and that inequality of possessions is inseparably connected with our present social system. From this it will follow that the present state of things cannot be remedied unless we change at once our whole social system; for, alter our form of government as we will, no such change can affect the system — no such change can prevent inequality of possessions, and the division of society into employers and employed —

and therefore, as a necessary consequence, no such change can remove the evils which this system and this division of society engender.

We do not act, and never yet have acted upon those First Principles which Nature has instituted for the guidance and the welfare of man; nor do we keep the broad principle of equality in view, either in our rights or our duties, our labors or our rewards. With us almost everything is unequal and unnatural and unjust. And why are things thus? How is it that some men receive only half allowance for doing double work, while others receive double or quadruple allowance merely for looking on? There is no principle in numbers which will enable one unaided man, with powers only equal to those of any other man, to perform the united labor of one hundred, — and there is no principle of reason or of justice which will allow one man to appropriate the fruits of the labor of one hundred. And yet this unjust appropriation has been practised and tolerated, in defiance of every principle of numbers and of justice, from the creation of man to the present day. Such is the operation of the present social system; on fraud and robbery legalized, stand all its power and wealth and glory; and until this system be overthrown, and immutable principles of right established, let no man speak of peace, or look for justice, or hope for happiness.

WOMAN'S RIGHTS.

If there are any rights withheld from women by our present social or civil rules, or if there are any privileges which could be accorded to them without affecting public morality and well-being let them be explained, restored, and granted.

It is so common to speak of woman as a perfect nonentity, — a mere accident in the race, — a sort of hot-bed exotic, cultivated more for show than for use, that we hardly know how to speak otherwise of her. But we can tell our conservative friends that in this matter they have not a particle of ground to stand upon, — not a peg upon which to hang an argument against this one simple fact: that woman is of the race an integral portion, subject to all social, civil, and criminal laws, yet without a direct voice in the matter. The direct civil and political isolation and exclusion of the chattel slaves of the South was not more complete than is that of woman in the most advanced state of what is recognized as the highest civilization. Every step taken by society towards her political emancipation is spoken of as a *favor* to the sex, and every such favor is regarded by some conservatives, as a wanton and unnecessary innovation upon wholesome laws. Why cannot these fearful and we fear somewhat fusty old bachelors, reflect that many such innovations were necessary before woman emerged from the degradation of savage life to her present state; and no more positive and absolute sign of progress is indicated in humanity, than the occasional abolition of those customs which consigned women to more than chattel slavery. We might refer to an old law of England, under which a man could put a rope round the neck of his wife, lead her to the marketplace, and there sell her to the highest bidder, precisely like a horse or a sheep. This rude and barbarous custom was but a symbol of the then prevailing idea of woman's sphere. She was regarded as a mere appendage to the race,— an instrument for man's lust and tyranny,— a sort of natural accident, resorted to by Nature on the spur of the moment, as a sort of necessary expedient to continue those lordly beings called *men*. No drudgery was too degrading for her to perform, no punishment too degrading for her crimes,— and that which was regarded in a gentleman as a mere peccadillo, unworthy of censure (licentiousness), was (and *is*) regarded in women as the last seal of utter social damnation.

To attempt to breathe a word in favor of injustice like this, so open, palpable, gross, is to waste breath, outrage common sense, and to justify wrong the most glaring. It matters nothing at all that the criminal law punishes their crimes with equal severity, nor can a conservative find a particle of countenance from this. Public opinion pronounces woman a social slave, and on the strength of this decree, every possible distinction is made between the same crime of the unmarried woman and man, — and the distinction is wholly against her. Here is the injustice of the present infernal social custom.

We are not able to conceive of any radical change in the existing marriage custom (always excepting the present law of divorce), which would be an improvement. But we do believe that placing woman in her proper political position would lead to a radical change in public opinion respecting her value. Either a woman is no whit above a horse, in the political and civil scale, or she is part and parcel of society, entitled to her voice and vote and property.

Marriage differs from business copartnerships, but it is a copartnership, nevertheless, and if any distinction be made in favor of either party, it should be for the weaker party; now, it is against her. Her labor, also, comes in for its share of degradation, and that labor which, performed by man, receives one hundred and fifty cents, when performed by woman receives about fifty or sixty cents.

These are *abuses*, the errors of past ignorance, and it is a sign of stultification not to reform them out of sight altogether.

SOCIETY.

Were man a stationary being, like the beasts and birds by which he is surrounded — had he a fixed and unchangeable instinct, instead of a progressive and improvable reason — any change in his social institutions would be unnecessary. Society would have been the same at the beginning, as it is at present; and it would continue one uniform state as long as man should exist. But man is not thus stationary; he is a reasoning, and therefore a progressive being. The knowledge and experience of one generation can be transmitted to the next; and, as a man at forty years of age must possess more knowledge than he did at twenty, so also must the world at large possess a greater accumulation of knowledge, at the end of four thousand years from the creation of man, than was possessed at the end of four hundred. Knowledge is simply an accumulation of facts; and wisdom is the art of applying such knowledge to its true purpose — the promotion of human happiness. Although men may have much knowledge, and no wisdom, there can only be little wisdom where there is but little knowledge. The present generation have the accumulated knowledge and experience of four thousand years to work upon: and therefore they have it in their power to act wiser, in respect to the establishment of social and political institutions, than any generation that has preceded them.

Such being the nature of man, and such his powers, the consideration of a social change need excite no more surprise or apprehension than a simple political movement. If a social change be a gigantic one, so, likewise, are the evils mighty which require to be removed. Throughout the whole universe, from the most stupendous planet to the individual atom, changes are perpetual, there is nothing at rest, nothing stationary; to affirm, therefore, that governmental institutions require no reformation, that social systems need no alteration, is just as absurd as to say that the man shall wear the swaddling clothes which befitted his infancy, and be pleased in maturity, with the rattle which charmed his childhood.

THE SCHOOLMASTER.

The position of the schoolmaster should be better secured. It is essential that he should be independent and respectable. His authority should be jealously guarded. His emoluments should be dealt with a liberal hand, and with an assured regularity, such as will place him beyond anxiety on that score, and thus leave his mind calm and free for an occupation in which calmness and freedom of mind are eminently requisite. A common blunder in this country is, to underrate the functions and importance of the schoolmaster. We buy our teachers in what is pecuniarily, though not in reality, the cheapest market. And yet we prate about our immortal souls! All the while neglecting or only half appreciating those whose influence must develop the capacity of knowledge into actual intelligence, and render the soul or mind more dignified and valuable than the instinct of the brute. Education has no more important problem to be solved than that of raising the educator to a proper position; that, we mean, which the well-being of the young and of society requires he should occupy.

PRIESTS.

The idea of going to heaven through the aid of priests places mankind at once in a stage of dependence and inferiority. When once accustomed to this state, they are thus necessarily prepared for all those degrading concessions and compliances, which constitute the condition of master and slave. Firmness and nobleness of mind are gone; men become dastards in character, and recreant in nature. The designing and hypocritical, who believe nothing of the imposition, join in the practice of it, to carry their own worldly schemes; some of pride, some of genius, others of gain, but like all schemes of tyranny, the burthen of paying and fighting for them falls invariably on the common mass.

It is impossible that the honest portion of the

community could for a moment maintain this system, if once brought to see its falsity. The whole system has been believed and adopted without a particle of proof; and that under the most unaccountable circumstances of absurdity and contradiction. Why do not honest men first demand proof of it, before they become its slaves. It is true that all systems of faith and religion are got up by man, to impose on his fellow; or it is true that one or more of them are instituted by deity. If any one be instituted by deity, which one is it? when was it instituted? where was it instituted? why was it instituted? No mark is put upon any known system by which it can be distinguished as coming from deity; on the contrary, all bear the mark of the folly and imperfection of man. If deity has designated any one system, no man has yet discovered this divine designation; all pretend to have it, however much opposed to each other, which is sufficient evidence that none has it.

FREE DISCUSSION.

The man not imbued with superstitions, and who entertains a sincere desire to promote the happiness of the human race, will readily admit, that open and impartial discussion is the foundation of human liberty. Free, unrestrained inquiry on all subjects, is, in fact, the source of knowledge and wisdom; for how can we detect error, or distinguish truth, if there is one topic remaining which we are not to investigate? We may expatiate for centuries on the advantages attending correct views and correct principles; but if those systems which brutalize the mind, which proscribe the use of reason, and which hold mankind under the dominion of a vile superstition, are not to be probed to the bottom, and exhibited in all their deformity, the most powerful eloquence, the most transcendent reasoning in the world (though of weight in their proper place) will be utterly useless. To convince man that happiness is attainable, it is not enough that he *know* this. The *causes* which deprive him of it, the *sources* of his misery, must be clearly and distinctly pointed out; otherwise, he will remain all his lifetime a child of sorrow and misfortune. Ignorant of the *nature* of the evils which beset him, he will continue the dupe of the crafty and designing, whose sole object it is to darken the understanding, that they may perpetuate their inordinate power and influence.

THE TRIUMPH OF LEARNING.

Mind constitutes the majesty of man; virtue, his true nobility. The tide of improvement which is now flowing through the land, like another Niagara, is destined to roll on downward to the latest posterity; and it will bear them on its bosom, our virtues, our vices, our glory, or our shame, or whatever else we may transmit as an inheritance. It, then, in a great measure, depends upon the present, whether the moth of immorality, of ignorance, and the vampire of luxury shall prove the overthrow of the republic, or knowledge and virtue, like pillars, shall support her against the whirlwind of war, ambition, corruption, and the remorseless tooth of time. Give your children fortune without education, and at least half the number will go down to the tomb of oblivion — perhaps to ruin. Give them education, and they will accumulate fortunes; they will be a fortune to themselves and their country. It is an inheritance worth more than gold, for it buys true honor. It can never be lost or spent, and through life it proves a friend; in death, a consolation. Give your children education, and no tyrant will trample over your liberties. Give your children education, and the silver-shod horse of the despot will never trample in ruins the fabric of your freedom.

HINTS TO HERETICS.

Be courageous. Dare to be honest, just, magnanimous, true to your country, to yourselves, to the world. Dare to do to others as you would have them do to you. Most men are cowards. They are afraid to speak and to act when duty calls, and as duty requires. Few men will suffer themselves to be called cowards; and yet they betray their cowardice by the very course they take to resent the insult. A man may intrepidly face the cannon's mouth, and be an arrant coward after all.

There is a higher, a nobler courage, than was ever displayed in the heat of battle, or on the field of carnage. There is a *moral* courage, which enables a man to triumph over foes more formidable than were ever marshalled by any Cæsar. A courage which impels him to do his duty, to hold fast his integrity, to maintain a conscience void of offence, at every hazard and sacrifice, in defiance of the world. Such is the courage that sustains every good man, amidst the temptations, allurements, honors, conflicts, opposition, ridicule, malice, cruelty, or persecution, which beset and threaten him at every stage of his progress through life.

THE THEATRE.

One of the most odious features of the Christian superstition is persecution; and one of the most reprehensible of its acts of continued vengeance is its persecution of the THEATRE. From time immemorial it has been at deadly war with it. At one time in the reign of the "Roundheads," in the days of Oliver Cromwell, than whom a more profound and painted hypocrite never lived, the stage was entirely suppressed; and if any one would enjoy a theatrical piece, he had to do it at his private house, at his own expense or that of his friends. Actors were as good as proscribed and banished England. The labors of eminent men, and even the works of the immortal Shakespeare, were suffered to lie among the rubbish of musty libraries, while the efforts of drivelling sermonizers and poetasters were read, rehearsed, and listened to, with avidity. We are not about to write an eulogy upon the stage, but we reprobate that poor, miserable, contracted spirit, which tries to drive people into an absurd superstition by excluding them from every species of amusement and innocent pastime, and by confining them eternally to the noise, confusion, rant and nonsense of a conventicle. But this is the only way that religionists can succeed.

. . . .

This much, however, we will say in behalf of the stage, and we challenge any one of intelligence and truth to deny its verity. The stage has ever preceded and accompanied refinement in manners, purity of taste, and a revival of literature and of the arts and sciences. Its most splendid triumphs have been in the presence of the most enlightened and freest governments. Tyrants of all kinds have been the first to fear and denounce the stage, unless indeed they could prostitute it to their interests. Some of the most distinguished men, men of the greatest rarity and most masterly talents, and men of sterling principles too, have written for it and considered their success, as it truly was, the pledge of their immortal fame. Mankind require amusement, relaxation and easy excitement of mind and feeling, and in some way or other they will have them; and the theatre in all large cities and towns present them on a large and rational scale, and cheaper than they can be obtained in any other way. When it is encouraged by the wise and good, it is raised up to a pure atmosphere, and, as a mirror, becomes bright, while left to the dregs of society, it becomes obscene by the polluted breath breathed upon it, proving, incontestibly, that like all other great vehicles of instruction, it is merely passive, ever a source of pleasure and of moral and intellectual profit as it is employed.

WHO IS AN ATHEIST?

Men tremble at the very name of an atheist. But who is an atheist? The man who brings mankind back to reason and experience, by destroying prejudices inimical to their happiness; who has no need of resorting to supernatural powers in explaining the phenomena of nature.

It is madness, say the theologians, to suppose incomprehensible motives in nature. Is it madness to prefer the known to the unknown? to consult experience and the evidence of our senses? to address ourselves to reason, and prefer her oracles to the decision of sophists who even confess themselves ignorant of the God they announce?

When we see priests so angry with atheistical opinions, should we not suspect the justice of their cause? Spiritual tyrants! 'tis ye who have defamed the divinity by besmearing him with the blood of the wretched! *You* are the truly impious! Impiety consists in insulting the God in whom it believes. He who does not believe in a God cannot injure him, and cannot of course be impious.

On the other hand, if piety consists in serving our country, in being useful to our fellow-creatures, and in observing the laws of nature, an atheist is pious, honest, and virtuous when his conduct is regulated by the laws which reason and virtue prescribe to him.

It is true, the number of atheists is inconsiderable, because enthusiasm has dazzled the human mind, and the progress of error has been so great that few men have courage to search for truth. If by atheists are meant those who, guided by experience and the evidences of their senses, see nothing in nature but what really exists; if by atheists are meant natural philosophers, who think everything may be accounted for by the laws of motion, without having recourse to a chimerical power; if by atheists are meant those who know not what a spirit is, and who reject a phantom, whose opposite qualities only disturb mankind, — doubtless there are many atheists; and their number would be greater, were the knowledge of physics and sound reason more generally disseminated.

An atheist does not believe in the existence of a God. No man can be certain of the existence of an inconceivable being, in whom inconsistent qualities are said to be united. In this sense many theologians would be atheists, as well as those credulous beings who prostrate themselves before a being of whom they have no other idea than that given them by men, avowedly comprehending nothing of him themselves.

TEMPERANCE.

As the habit of drinking ardent spirits is injurious to the human constitution, and as the man who indulges in it runs great risk of becoming sooner or later a confirmed inebriate, since moderate drinking is the downhill road to intemperance, we would sincerely caution every one who has not yet contracted the habit, to be on his guard against it, and would earnestly advise every one who is indulging in drink as a beverage, to abstain from it altogether. We have not a word to say in disparagement of the men who drink. They are often found among the best men in the community; and, knowing this fact, and feeling sorry to see them injuring themselves by a hurtful habit, we throw out our caution and advice as a matter of duty.

We are well aware, however, that mere advice and caution are not enough to prevent intemperance to any great extent. Something more is needed, and when that is found out, we shall make a great deal more progress in suppressing the evil than we now do. Notwithstanding all that has been written and said upon the subject of intemperance, we have an idea that the philosophy of the habit is but very little understood even yet — we mean by this, the causes that make intemperance, and the means to remove it. Intemperance, as a general thing, being an artificial or an acquired habit, it would seem as if the right understanding of the laws of our nature would suggest a natural, harmless and effectual preventative.

But how will you prevent intemperance? Probably the answer that we should give to this question would satisfy but a small part of the community; in fact, most of the people might look upon our remedy as worse than the disease, so much are people governed by prejudice, and opposed to innovation. Yet we shall venture to throw out a few hints, in the hope that they may reach some liberal and common-sense minds qualified to judge, and not afraid to avow publicly their convictions

Our plan would be to regenerate the people — teach them habits of temperance — provide them roomy dwelling-houses, and plenty of water; open up for them on Sunday, their most drunken day, every available means of rational enjoyment; give them every facility for innocent amusement and recreation; let them have free access to museums, exhibitions of the fine arts, reading-rooms, and every other conceivable means of innocently and rationally passing their time. Here is the answer to the question, "How will you prevent intemperance?"— *Provide a substitute for the bar-room.*

INDIVIDUAL EFFORT.

How little there is existing in society of what can be truly called individual effort! How rare the instance of a man depending solely on the influence of his own merit or moral worth, to insure success or preferment! But perhaps this deficiency of character nowhere appears so strongly marked as in the conduct which governs many in their social intercourse. We there see the young man, — who ought of all others to rely on his own desert alone for promotion and reward, — manifesting a desire to advance by the meritorious deeds of others.

The patriotic services or great possessions of a father, for example, are ofttimes considered by the son as entitling *him* to acceptance and renown, as if he had a right to wear the laurels that value or industry alone has gained for another. It is his duty, and should be his pride, to preserve and defend those laurels from blight and aspersion; but it is sacrilegious in the extreme, to rob the dead of honors they bore while living. Rather let the son be the artificer of his own fortune. Let him carve out his own way, dependent only on his own exertions, and trusting only to them for what the future may make him. Then, when success has perfected what real merit began, he can rest his claims for admiration and applause, on a basis sure and permanent, and one on which diligence and worth will have raised a superstructure honorable to his memory.

> "What merit to be dropped on fortune's hill?
> The honor is to *mount it*."

HEAVEN AND HELL.

What evidence is there of the existence of these places, in the view in which professing Christians generally, take of them? We never could find any: and one sect, at least, the Universalists, appear to have been quite as unsuccessful as regards the latter place, as ourselves. They have long since exploded the idea of any such place as hell. But would they not find it just as difficult to prove any such place as heaven? People have no more come back to tell us anything about heaven, than they have to tell us about hell. We may say that people have dreamed about it; so they have dreamed about the other place just as much.

The only idea, therefore, that we can form either of heaven or hell, exists in the mind, and there only — it is a state, and not a place — that such is the fact, is obvious from daily experience and common observation; and let theologians mystify and speculate as they will, the true doctrine is simply this: *Happiness is Heaven; and the misery which arises from guilt is Hell.*

RELIGIOUS DESPOTISMS.

It appears that the constitutions of antiquity were as inimical to religious freedom as modern governments, and that conformity of opinion has at no time been obtained except by the terror of penal statutes.

An absolute freedom in discussing religion, has never yet existed in any age or country. The religion of Athens was interwoven with its constitution, and neither genius, learning, courage, nor the softer virtues, uncombined with the superstition of the age, could screen their possessors from the persecutions of an implacable priesthood. Among the Romans, too, it was toleration, not freedom.

It was in vain, however that those mighty authorities endeavored to fetter the transmission of thought, and to fix the opinions of the human race. Man, though individually confined to a narrow spot, and limited in his existence to a few courses of the sun, has, nevertheless an imagination which ranges into the infinities of space, and the ever-rolling current of ages. The petty legislators of the hour issue their mandates that a boundary shall be drawn around the energy of mind, — " Thus far shalt thou go, but no farther." Such is the fiat, but it is as useless as that which would restrain the waves of the ocean. Time, that successfully consigns to oblivion the ever-changing governments and religions of men, and which now sits upon the ruins of despotic Greece and Rome, — their temples despoiled of their deities and crumbled into dust, — will as surely destroy the sacred despotisms that have tyrannized over mankind, now too long, under the symbols of the crescent and the cross.

CONSCIENCE.

Conscience is no more than the effect of reasoning or passing ideas, either upon past scenes or upon present appearances. It is thus, when the ideas are caused by the recollection of past actions, that our sense of right and wrong, our reason or conscience, either acquits or condemns it. It is a reasoning on the ideas then present; and it is the same thing, the same process, whether it be an action of our own, or that of another, on the probability or improbability of what we are told being true; or on the causes of the effect we see surrounding us.

Many men will pass through life without ever making any use of their reason, beyond the best method of getting money and how to enjoy it, leaving all the rest unknown or unheeded.

Others think it is enough to do as they are ordered, and believe in religion only because the priests require it. But it is a different, a widely different case, with the philosophizing part of mankind; they reason on every subject that sends an idea to the mind, they are continually seeking after truth, and exposing falsehood; obtaining knowledge that therewith they may better the condition of themselves and their fellow-men; protecting and teaching the practice of morality, as the only method calculated to make men free and happy, and exposing the errors of religion as being the most hostile to their welfare and improvement.

TO ADVOCATE UNWELCOME TRUTHS NO EASY TASK.

It is far easier to swim with the tide of popular approbation, and to "echo the million" than to stand forth as a solitary unit, and advocate an opinion unwelcome in its aspect to the general corruption of popular sentiment. It is less difficult "to fall heirs to our opinions," and to defend them as people do their estates, by right of inheritance, than to institute an inquiry, examine their character, and, according as that inquiry and examination may direct us, to reject or adopt them with an honest yet fearless discrimination.

AGITATION.

There is a large class of people in the community who always oppose the agitation of any new question or doctrine. They are sure that some terrible calamity will follow the advent of a newly established measure in social or political government. They view a new doctrine with fear and distrust.

Who are these non-agitators? We shall find them the least enterprising and the least useful folks in the world. If their fathers believed in witches, hell-fire, and cloven feet, ten to one, those people who are afraid of agitation, believe in the same dogmas and follies. They are content to be governed by the same laws, satisfied with the same station in life, and thankful for as much liberty as their ancestors enjoyed, without asking any questions or causing any agitation. They enjoy life in the same way that an alligator enjoys a cold winter, by virtue of pure stupidity.

The fact is, we owe every improvement of the age, every advance in science, government, and art, to agitation. It lies at the foundation of all human good. Revolutions and republics trace their origin to this source; liberty of thought and of speech are greatly its debtor, and freedom of conscience was established through its influence. We have nothing to fear from agitation, but everything to fear from stagnation. The former denotes intellectual life: the latter, mental death. If republicanism ever becomes degenerated in America, it will ensue from stagnation in the public mind, brought on by selfishness and luxury. It is of the utmost importance, then, that exciting topics of public interest be constantly kept in view, and discussed, not only in regard to our own country, but also of other nations.

The interest of Americans in the affairs of Europe is increasing every day, and this interest, through agitation, will soon be felt and appreciated by the masses of the Europeans, who will the sooner strike for their liberties. Keep up agitation. It is the watchword of freedom. Keep it up.

OPINIONS.

In no case can man be justly rewarded or punished for his opinions; they originate not in the will, but in the understanding: they are involuntary and not criminal. When the mind perceives a sufficient reason or cause for believing a proposition, it is evident it must believe it; it would be absurd to say one had seen a sufficient reason for believing a statement and could not believe it; on the other hand, when the mind perceives a reason or cause for believing a proposition untrue, the mind must believe it untrue because it has seen a sufficient reason for it.

The truth of these observations is evident from the absurdity that would follow the contrary supposition, which would be to admit that the mind was capable of perceiving a proposition to be false, while at the same time it concluded it to be true; or of disbelieving what it had reason to believe. Here it is evident that belief of any kind, or unbelief of any kind, does not imply moral guilt. We must believe what our judgment tells us is true, disbelieve what our judgment tells us is untrue, and doubt what our judgment has not perceived sufficient reason for believing to be either true or false.

There is no crime without a breach of some moral law; but here there is no breach of any moral law, but the fulfilment of an imperious law of nature, which impels us to disbelieve what we do not see reason for believing.

EXAGGERATION.

If there be any habit that is universal among mankind, it is that of coloring too highly the things that we describe. We cannot be content with a simple relation of truth; we must exaggerate, we must have "a little too much red in the brush." Whoever heard of a dark night that was not "pitch dark," of a strong man that was not as "strong as a horse," or a miry road that was not "up to the knee"? We would walk fifty miles on foot to see the man who never caricatures a subject on which he speaks. But where is such a man to be found? "From rosy morn to dewy eve," in our conversation we are constantly outraging truth. If somewhat wakeful in the night, "we scarcely had a wink of sleep"; if our sleeves get a little damp in a shower, "we are as wet as if dragged through a brook"; if a breeze blows up while we are in the harbor, the waves are sure to "run mountains high"; and if a man grows rich, we all say, "he rolls in money." No later than yesterday, a friend, who would shrink from wilful misrepresentation, told us hastily as he passed, that the "newspaper had nothing in it but advertisements."

THE QUESTION.

The question to decide is, Are we really to be a republic, actually a free people, — free as Nature, — free to reason, — free to speak the truth? Is there to be a nation on the earth where the rights of humanity can truly be enjoyed? where a Socrates, who exposed the tyrannical shackles imposed by the effect of the vulgarly established religious prejudices, would not be subjected to religious murder? Are Americans to be a free, intelligent, moral, and philosophic people, or are they to be merely a Christian people, to continue always under the bonds of the Christian superstition?

Is the country always to continue a mere Christian hierarchy, made to answer the ends of a set of Christian priests? Is belief in future rewards and punishments to be sustained as law? Is the abominable Christian test oath to be continued a *sine qua non* for obtaining civil justice? and are conscientious men, who vindicate the truth of everlasting nature, to be none but outlaws? Let the question be answered.

THE PRESENT AGE.

The influence of a more rational education is beginning to be felt; the darkness of superstition and bigotry, which has so long shrouded the minds of men, is gradually wearing away; enlightenment is constantly augmenting, and knowledge is destined at no very distant day "to cover the earth as the waters cover the channel of the great deep." Yet there are those who, instead of rejoicing, seem to mourn at these things — these cheering symptoms which speak to us of a brighter day. Surely that man's greatness cannot be founded on true and just principles which cannot stand the light of knowledge and the careful investigation of intelligent minds.

Educate the people, and you subvert tyranny. The people are the source of all political and social power, and if to this be added the power which knowledge can confer, who or what will be able to withstand them?

The present age is one big with important events, and the state of that man's mind is not to be envied who can view with cool and careless indifference the changing circumstances of the present day. And yet many sneer at the social and political struggles of the poor man, who imagine that he might be better occupied in attending to his daily labor, than in examining into and meddling with the affairs of state and society. But surely every man who is governed has a right to know how he is governed; and it must certainly be a government of very doubtful character which cannot admit of the examination of any of its subjects. All forms of political and social administration should progress with the progressing times, and a law which has governed a community in the days of its comparative ignorance cannot, without danger, be enforced when that community has attained to anything like social and moral eminence.

Has the American nation made such an advancement? And if so, has the American government advanced in a proportionate degree? It remains for the American people themselves to answer these questions! If legislation be oppressive, if there be corruptions that might be eradicated, if there be new and better laws that might be framed, let not the people cease their struggles till error be vanquished and truth triumphant. They may be opposed, and they will be opposed, for the hand of the oppressor is never weary, but if they stand firmly and combat bravely, the desired end will ultimately be gained. The words of Byron, —

> "Methinks I hear a little bird that sings
> The people bye and bye will be the stronger"—

are fast fulfilling like a prophecy; and we most sincerely bid *lightning speed* to every effort that is made to advance the important cause of social and political liberty.

THOMAS PAINE.

Thomas Paine was a great apostle of liberty; a bold and fearless enemy of kings and princes; a sterling, uncompromising, unflinching advocate of the rights of man, and one of the master-spirits of the American Revolution.

It may be reasonably doubted whether our Revolution could have succeeded, at that particular time, had the pen of Thomas Paine taken no part in the contest; had he not have written "Common Sense" to bring on the war, and the various numbers of the "Crisis" to push it through to a glorious and triumphant termination.

Priestcraft has almost entirely destroyed the reputation of this great patriot; and we may learn from this fact the exceeding virulence of the enemy with which we contend. Had Thomas Paine never written against priestcraft, a national monument would probably have been erected to his memory, and we tremble for the safety of the republic when we think of the success of the clergy's endeavors to extinguish the fame of this celebrated man. When we forget the men who gave us our liberty, we shall soon forget that priestcraft and kingcraft are the enemies of liberty, and so we shall become a willing prey. Shall it be said that the friends and martyrs of liberty must be sacrificed in this country to dignify a parson's discourse? Forbid it, justice! Forbid it, all ye who claim the proud title of American citizen!

SELF-RESPECT.

One of the strongest and most prevalent incentives to virtue is the desire of the world's esteem. We act right, rather that our actions may be applauded by others, than to have the approbation of our own conscience. We refrain from doing wrong not so much from principle, as from the fear of incurring the censure of the world. A due regard ought, indeed, to be paid to public opinion, but there is a regard we owe ourselves, of far greater importance, a regard which keeps us from committing a wrong action when withdrawn from the observation of the world, as much as when exposed to its broad glare. If we are as good as others, why stand in more fear of others than of ourselves? What is there in other men that makes us desire their approbation, and fear their censure, more than our own? In other respects we are apt to overrate ourselves, but surely when we pay such blind and servile respect to the opinions of others, we forget our own dignity, and undervalue ourselves in our own esteem. We admire the sentiment of Cassius when, speaking of the imperial Cæsar, he exclaims:

> "I had as lief not be, as live to be
> In awe of such a thing as I myself."

The great slight the men of sense who have nothing but sense; the men of sense despise the great, who have nothing but greatness; and the honest man pities them both, if, having greatness or sense only, they have no virtue.

SECTARIANISM.

There is a powerful influence at work, which acts like an electrical element of discord, repelling with fiery vehemence the efforts of philanthropists and reformers. It is *sectarianism*, and it produces a state of things which brings dishonor on the country. It wastes in paltry contests the mental energy that should be applied in improving the moral, intellectual, and social condition of the people; it stifles their emotions of benevolence and justice; consumes their substance in building chapels and salarying priests; and, worst of all, it renders them moral cowards; for so intense and active is sectarian hostility, and so vindictive is its spirit, that thousands who see and deplore these evils are deterred from attempting to remove them.

They occasion more evil still. They prevent the development of the national mind. In our universities and schools they direct and control and cramp the aspirations of the student. The catechism and confession of faith are thrust between him and external creation; he must draw his theology from them; and small encouragement is given to him to gather truths from the magnificent stores of Nature. The standards of the church and they chiefly, must constitute his religious and moral belief; if he acquires any other doctrines, it must be at his peril and by stealth. In short, the teaching of Nature is nearly unknown; nay, it is frowned upon, is stigmatized as "Infidel," and the catechism is thrust into the reluctant hands of the teacher, to be taught in its place.

There are two questions, wholly distinct, which here suggest themselves.

The first one is of a religious nature — "What shall I do to be saved?" This, every man is at liberty, in the exercise of an unquestionable right, to judge of, and answer for himself.

Whether it is a momentous subject or not, no one has the prerogative to dictate to another what he shall believe in regard to it; and the sect that thus intrudes itself between a man and his conscience is meddling with what it has no concern.

The other question, which is the *Great Question*, is: "What shall we do to provide wholesome food, comfortable raiment, pleasant dwellings, and the harmless luxuries of life, for the poor and indigent?" This question, *the* question in fact, of the age — the catechism does not answer.

Sectarianism which relates wholly to an unseen and unknown world, does little or nothing for social elevation and improvement. The means for this great consummation consist of rational education and better circumstances; when these are enjoyed by the poor and overworked laboring classes, they will rise to the dignity of intelligent beings, and cease to wage the hopeless war of competition with the steam engine and the horse.

THE WORKING CLASS.

If the working class had always been as enlightened as any other class of the community, is it not certain that the institutions of society, framed and established under the influence of such enlightenment, would have been calculated to promote their interests at least, equally with the interests of any other class of the community?

They alone were the producers of wealth; they were always superior in numbers; what then could it be but *want of intelligence* that disabled them from demanding the formation and establishment of institutions which would make *them* who were the only producers, the proprietors and enjoyers of at least as great a share of the proceeds of their own industry, as any others?

Here then is the root of the evil: those who controlled their destinies were more informed than they. Superior information gave them superior power; and having a direct interest in accumulating the products of other people's labor, (themselves being exempt therefrom) and thus of subjecting the working classes to endless toil, they were induced and enabled by such degrees as each succeeding state of society would admit, to frame and establish institutions, the almost invariable result of which is to render poverty-stricken and degraded the condition of the producer, while they enrich and aggrandize the indolent consumer. Here then we discover the *main cause* of the degradation that ever has, and ever will assail the workingmen, so long as they continue the lamentable subjects of it, and one which nothing can remove but a general diffusion of knowledge through the working class, and an unreserved dissemination of truth, particularly in relation to *equal rights and moral and political economy.*

REFORMERS.

One of the most common errors of mankind (says the Brooklyn Eagle) is the confidence which is reposed in organizations to cherish and promote reforms. They look to the regular schools of medicine for reforms in the practice of medicine; to the regular schools of divinity for a proper construction of all questions of morals; and to the apostles of science for the true theories of all natural laws. And yet it would seem that all great discoveries, great reforms, and great developments of truth have been resisted by the schools, and have made their way against the prejudices of those who should have been their promoters, but who, blinded by their interests, or the conservative influence of the schools, have been unable to perceive the truth, and have stood like a rock against it.

The great movements of the world have generally commenced among those who were apparently the least calculated to advance them; among those who were weak in power and influence. The advocates of political liberty are not the powerful princes and barons, who could, if they chose, establish it at once and without struggle or bloodshed. Christianity began in the family of a poor mechanic and was rejected by priests and rulers and the great doctors of its early days. The great reformation began with a poor monk, and was resisted by the Church, which was organized on purpose to promote purity in doctrine, and purity in morals. The late reforms under Wesley and Whitfield, and the strict notions of the reformers were ridiculed, and their persons held in contempt and subjected to insult; and the discoverer of the true movements of the heavenly bodies, the discoverer of the circulation of the blood, and the discoverer of the true theory of storms, all had the mortification to see their great ideas rejected by the world of science.

Questions of right cannot be settled, therefore, by the *ipse dixit* of the schoolmen, or high officers of state, or distinguished magnates in the walks of science. Truth is constantly battling with error, and those who fight against it the hardest are generally its sworn ministers. The great reformer of Nazareth was put to death by the orthodox doctors of his day, for his heresies; and since his time, a whole army of martyrs have suffered for believing doctrines which in later times have come to be received as settled axioms.

These things teach us caution in deciding on anything new. The worst tribunal to which an *outside* truth can be submitted, is the regular school. Your true schoolman rejects everything which is not in his books, and frowns on all new discoveries which do not originate with his party.

LIBERTY.

Liberty is an old word, but of changeable meaning. Not many years ago it had a very limited sense. That nation was supposed to possess liberty that was uncontrolled by any other. In 1776 it took a wider meaning, and implied not only national independence, but a right to choose our own form of government and select our own rulers. The victory we gained was to secure this liberty to the world. This was a giant stride in the march of human emancipation. Man seemed in this mighty leap to have outstripped himself; and considering what he had been, what he is now in most countries, it is not strange that his achievements appeared almost incredible. But, by a close inspection, with the eye of the philosopher, of the philanthropist, we shall easily discover that we then only gained the starting-point, merely opened the lists to human reason and human perfectibility.

Liberty has yet a wider sense — one vastly more important than national independence, or the right to choose our own government and rulers. With these, man is but half free. There is a more subtile and a more powerful tyrant that lurks within and enslaves the mind. Religion, custom, habit, influence of wealth, of some adventitious circumstance, may make or keep the many vassals to the few. Men thus circumstanced are the veriest slaves that live. There are no chains like those which fetter the mind. There must be MENTAL as well as *political* liberty. The timid slave of custom may be a vile minion of power, and make his body a footstool for the aspiring demagogue to clamber into office; but it belongs not to such as he to detect, seize, and secure the rights of man. Genuine Republicanism must rest on MENTAL LIBERTY, or it will have neither beauty nor permanence.

MOTIVES.

It is the motive, more than anything else, that renders an action good or bad. However fair the appearance of an action may be, if the right motive be wanting, the action is hollow; if the motive be a bad one, the action is rotten to the core. Who cares for an outward seeming, or show of affection unless the heart be also on the same terms? Who does not prize a rough outside, when it covers an honest inside, more than the most fawning fondness from a heart that is cold and false? Thus it is right to insist on the principles for their own sake, because the principles give their value to the action, not the action to the principles, for they are but dross. The principles are the gold on which is to be placed the stamp, and if the gold is not good, the stamp, though it often deceives the people, gives it no real worth; as he who graves the queen's image on base metal is punished for his forgery.

VIRTUE AND RELIGION.

We have no idea of permitting any man, who assumes the garb of piety, to claim, in consequence, any preëminence in virtue. We prize truth above all things, and it is quite time that we understood the just distinction between virtue and religion.

We consider, then, that religion is not even presumptive evidence of virtue. Religion is a belief in a superintending Providence, who is swerved by prayer, and who yields to the supplications of the penitent. This belief is compatible, as all experience teaches, with great moral obliquity in the same individual, or it may unite with great virtue in the same person. Religion, therefore, offers no proof of a good life, but it is evidence of great selfishness. God or Nature has made self-interest the rule of action in man; to say that a man acts without self-interest is to say that he moves without a motive power. The broad, natural distinction, therefore, — all men being equally selfish, — between virtue and vice, that distinction which is founded in the nature of things, we take to be this: the virtuous man pursues his self-interest, his self-gratification, so as never to invade the rights of others, and to administer as much to the happiness of his fellows as lies in his power; the vicious man pursues his self-interest, his self-gratification, regardless of the rights and interests of his fellows.

If this definition be founded in nature, it follows that religion is not evidence of virtue. The religious man works for his reward, and, like the adventurous merchant, makes a long investment; he is willing to endure much here for the benefit of the long and happy hereafter, which lies in prospect. Let us, then, take religious people as we find them; try them by their conduct towards mankind, and not by their belief, or by their rites towards their God. If you find a kind, benevolent, just-dealing man, call him what he is — a virtuous, good citizen. If you see an intolerant, egotistical, vain, persecuting man, though he beat the pulpit for a living, and pray loud at conference meetings, class him among the vicious — it is his natural rank.

BAD INTENTIONS.

It is in the power of the abusive to charge men with intentions which they never entertained — with motives which their hearts abhor. The innocent conduct of individuals may be easily misinterpreted, and such misinterpretation will be readily adopted by the prejudiced and unreflecting, who are ever willing to suit things to their own malignant purposes. It is wiser, then, for us, who declare the truth of everlasting Nature, by prudent, good, and regular conduct, to acquire such a character as will explain to the impartial observer, the purity of the motives by which we are actuated, in cases in which our views are ungenerously or maliciously misrepresented. We sacrifice our personal interests; we incur the rancor of clerical malice; we resign all that others prize as pleasures and advantages — for the sake of virtue, reason, and truth; and we enjoy a fecility unknown to the ignorant and superstitious.

THE WORLD MOVES.

States of society, and forms of government have always been forced upon men by the common march of events; and that state of society or form of government which existed at one period of a nation's history, and was sufficient for all its wants, will not be tolerated at a later period. Who, at the present day, would wish to return to a state of society, with its accompanying manners and form of government, and religious institutions, such as existed in Great Britain in the time of the Druids, or the Romans, or the Saxons, or the Normans? How many Protestants would wish to revive the days when Catholicism was in its glory and its power, and the brand of persecution dried up the blood of the martyrs?

These changes were but manifestations of the common progress of things, and they all happened naturally and unavoidably, independent of the control of governments or individuals. Catholicism succeeded Paganism; then Protestantism came after Catholicism, and both are now being superseded by Dissent; and all the evils which these changes brought upon the people of other days, as well as all the miseries that have befallen nations in our own times, are solely attributable to the insane and blasphemous endeavors of human rulers to set up their authority against Reason and Progress, and to tell man he shall go no farther.

And have all the treasures wasted and the blood spilled — all the persecutions and punishments and revolting crimes which have taken place to keep man and his institutions stationary, effected the object for which they were intended? Turn to history for an answer, — look back from our days, to the days of our forefathers, and ask if any of the many powerful endeavors to prevent changes, ever yet succeeded.

RELIGION AND LIBERALISM.

When the assertion is made that the Christian religion has always, from the day of its origin, been the promoter of strife and discord, the generality of men regard you with the stare of incredulity. They do not believe it, or cannot understand how it can be possible. They have always heard Christianity spoken of as the parent of peace and harmony; and they cannot for a moment imagine that she could ever in any way, directly or indirectly, support or countenance war or bloodshed. The assertion of the skeptic is denied with no little warmth, and he is pointed to this great Republic as a living refutation of his charge.

We have no religious wars here, but we are a Christian people, nevertheless, and therefore it is false to say that religion is the promoter of strife and contention.

True, we have no religious wars among us, but we are not quite certain that their absence is owing to the humanizing tendences of Christianity. We attribute it altogether to the increase of Mental Liberty, the offspring of Liberal or Infidel Principles; and to Political Liberty, the offspring of Republicanism.

Some two hundred years ago, when these saving principles were but imperfectly understood, or hardly understood at all, men and women were tortured and put to death in this country, for religion's sake. There was no lack of Christianity among those Pilgrim Fathers who instigated and carried out the frightful persecutions of their day — in fact they committed them under the guidance and direction of Christianity, as they understood it; and if Massachusetts was as religious at the present time, as she was when she hanged the Quakers for their religion, she would hang Quakers still.

But all this brutality has come to an end, and we now enjoy comparative freedom of conscience; and we owe the blessing entirely to the introduction and dissemination of Liberalism. It has stopped the taking of life for opinion's sake, and eventually, as it increases and becomes popular, will remove every species of persecution. But Christianity never did and never can, from its very nature, exercise this benevolent spirit, because its nature is bigotry. Give either of the two great denominations of Christians, Catholics, or Protestants, supreme **power, and** neither of **them would show any** mercy to dissenters. Their history confirms the truth of this assertion. They both have persecuted, and do still, to the extent they dare to go; and they would go farther were it not for the counteracting barrier of Liberalism, which lies like an impregnable mountain across their path. In our own country there is more Liberalism than in any other, and hence there is less persecution to be met with than in any other. But no thanks to Christianity for this superiority. It is all due to Liberalism, which, while it teaches the honest inquirer his rights and duties, stands a wall of defence to shield him from the remorseless vengeance of religious bigotry. Take away this shield, and let Christianity have no opposing force, and there would be nothing to save the doubter of to-day from experiencing the fate of the Quakers in the early times of New England.

Liberalism, not Christianity, is what has given us our free institutions and the degree of political and mental liberty we possess. The system of Christianity, which was originated some eighteen hundred years ago, may have been as good a one as the people to whom it was given were capable of appreciating; but as it neither allowed nor contemplated anything like improvement in its principles, it would seem to belong to another age, while Liberalism, gathering knowledge from the march of reason and the discoveries of science, is enabled to improve upon the past, and offer a system more in accordance with Truth and Nature.

SUNDAY SCHOOLS.

The early object of Sunday schools, why they were first established (in England) by Robert Raikes and kindred minds, was apparently a benevolent, not a religious object.

There were thousands of English children who were so constantly employed in labor during weekdays, that Sunday was the only day when they had any leisure to attend school. This day was usually spent by them in idleness, mischief, and vice. It was very important, therefore, that they should have an opportunity afforded for acquiring knowledge and good principles on the only day when the overwhelming avarice of the rich men of society could afford them any leisure. We have not the historical documents before us, and therefore cannot quote them; but these documents would show that the ostensible object of the originators of Sunday schools was benevolent and praiseworthy. Scarcely had these schools become general, before they were diverted from their original and proper object.

It was found that those poor children who had no time for attending school during the week, were needed as servants for another kind of labor on the Sabbath. The avarice of society would allow them no rest, even on the day of rest. But the Sabbath schools were found to be an excellent institution in the hands of the church and the priesthood, for extending their power and influence. Sermons, and the other usual services at church, produced but little effect upon the minds of children, and all the labor of this kind of teaching devolved upon the pastor. In the Sunday schools, on the contrary, children were made the special objects of attention, they could be instructed in that way which would be most agreeable to them; and the burden would be laid upon the shoulders of men and women, of various ages, who might be interested in the work, and ambitious for a little notoriety.

Thus were Sunday schools at length made universal; and so far has their original object been forgotten, that the children of the poor are hardly seen there, unless they are well instructed during the week, so as to be able and qualified to receive the religious instruction there given. If poor children cannot learn to read during the week, they cannot be taught to read at the Sunday school. Not by any means. Such instruction would be deemed by the pious hypocrites of the present day, as a profanation of the holy Sabbath. Christianity, however, is making its death-struggles. Its supporters are obliged to use every artifice that human ingenuity can invent to keep it alive. We shall soon be divided into Infidels and Catholics. Protestantism is fast running into Infidelity.

REVERENCE FOR OLD DOCTRINES.

Reverence for the opinions of one's ancestry is one of the most remarkable of all humbugs. It is not so much a natural sentiment as one industriously inculcated by the deceivers of men, as tending to promote the stability of all established errors, prejudices and pernicious customs. It is a doctrine very favorable to the permanency of aristocratic institutions, but fatal to Republicanism. Men are taught to identify themselves with their ancestors, that they may respect their prejudices, upon which the power of the privileged classes is established. For this reason they are taught to regard it as the greatest reproach to forsake their fathers' follies, superstitions, and errors.

That feeling which is most assiduously cherished in the tender mind is reverence. This is the humbug by which in later life men may be blindly led into subjection. They are taught to banish all self-reliance from their minds, to place no confidence in their own powers, but to rely solely upon the godliness and wisdom of those men who, from compassion for their natural inability to reason, have furnished them with leading-strings, that they may not go astray.

The first lesson which is taught to youth is reverence. His reverence and obedience are to compensate him for the sacrifice he has made of his reasoning powers and common-sense on the altar of superstition. He is taught to reverence the clergy — not for their virtues, for they may have no virtues — but to reverence their persons, and their opinions also. He is taught to reverence the instructors of his childhood, instructors always appointed through the influence of the clergy, that he may receive implicitly all the errors which hoodwinkers have established for their own interested purposes.

Men are taught to venerate the holy bandage which is placed over the eyes of their minds, and which disposes them piously to be guided by others, rather than to follow the wicked and blind guidance of their own natural reason. They are taught that the unpardonable sin would be to remove the bandage, which was placed over their eyes with the highest regard for their temporal and eternal good. Divested of this bandage, they would no longer reverence their errors and prejudices, and the pious authors of humbugs and diabolical deceptions; they would forsake religion and follow after the understanding of their own hearts, and in the ways of philosophy and common sense. They would prefer the light of their own minds to the darkness of superstition. Hence nothing so greatly offends the blindfolded people, no less than their hoodwinkers, as to witness a fellow-citizen declaring his mental independence, and shaking off his reverence for their blind guides.

COURAGE.

No man was ever truly great, no man ever accomplished great things, who did not possess tranquil, steadfast, immovable courage. When once an opinion is formed on good grounds, when once, after due reflection, a determination is taken, it should be persisted in at every hazard of personal consequence. It is better to fall than to bend; to be broken than to yield. This secures the respect and admiration of enemies, if not their approbation and concurrence. The opposite course is as impolitic as it is weak. Defeat then becomes disgrace; misfortune carries with it degradation. The wounds of the prostrate combatant are all in the back; his very scars are not those of honor, but of shame. To be weak is miserable. Discomfiture is more certain, and is sullied and aggravated by contempt. Nothing is ever gained by cowardice; nothing is ever achieved by concession as to principle. This but renders a triumphing foe more haughty, insolent, and relentless. The best way to avoid danger, as the Irishman said, is to meet it.

To a really elevated mind, opposition is but a stimulus to greater exertion, an incentive to more strenuous effort. What merit is there in a victory easily achieved? What glory is it to triumph over obstacles that are light, to overpower an enemy who is weak? Danger is the element of true greatness, the atmosphere in which it lives, and moves and has its being. Resistance but kindles the resolution of exalted courage. Obloquy, misrepresentation, prejudice, ignorance, envy, passion, these hideous shapes are mere phantoms which vanish before the glance of determination, and are at once exposed and laid open by a voice of power and intrepidity.

FREE SPEECH.

It is much to be lamented that too many people yet conceive that there are some opinions which ought not to be tolerated, as they imagine the free expression of them would tend to disorganize society, by subverting what they believe to be the foundation of virtue. How can any danger possibly arise from the unrestrained expression of any opinions whatever, where reason and truth are left free to combat them? It is time the world had done with such groundless apprehensions; they have been sources of infinite mischief in all ages, and in every country.

Such people breathe the very spirit of despotism, and wish to communicate it. It is impossible not to infer from their apprehensions, that, as men increase in knowledge, they must see reason to disapprove the systems established. How can that mind be constituted which contemplates the progress of human knowledge as matter of regret or fear? The wider the diffusion of knowledge, the better the people are informed, the more they understand — the more likely they are to see and comprehend what is for their good, and the means by which that good is to be attained; the more likely they are to abstain from such means as would be prejudicial in their operation, and calculated rather for the prevention than the attainment of that good.

THE CLOSING YEAR.

"Nothing is lasting on the world's wide stage,
As sung, and wisely sung, the Grecian sage;
And man, who through the globe extends his sway,
Reigns but the sovereign creature of a day.

One generation comes; another goes;
Time blends the happy with the man of woes;
A different face of things each age appears;
And all things alter in a course of years."

We are just now passing one of those milestones that mark the progress we have made in the journey of existence. The occasion suggests to us the inestimable value of TIME, which is given to man for his improvement. By the protraction of life, opportunities are afforded for our growth in knowledge and in usefulness. We were not raised into being, that we might be idle spectators of the objects with which we are surrounded. The situation in which we are placed demands reiterated exertion. The sphere in which we move calls for the putting forth all the ability with which we may be endowed.

Inquiries therefore should be made, how improvements can be best effected, either in our individual or social capacities. This conduct will reflect an honor on our rationality; this train of action will elevate us in the scale of being, and impart a zest to our enjoyment. It is said that the elder Cato repented of three things — and one of them was his having passed a day without improvement.

"We know not what to-morrow may bring forth"— and it is best for us that we do not. The anticipation of our joys or of our griefs is often a burden too heavy to be borne. Pretentions, indeed, are made to a knowledge of our future destiny; but the imposition has been detected and exposed. Our wisest way is to throw the reins over a vain curiosity. Contented with that portion of information which is commensurate with our faculties, and congenial with our present situation, let us devote our knowledge to the benefit of humanity, and resolve that before we — "Bid the working world good-night," we will make it some better for our having lived in it.

THE UNKNOWN.

It is rather a singular fact, that, taking mankind as we find them, they appear to be confident of some things in proportion as they are ignorant of them.

The "next world" is one of these things. Who *knows* anything concerning it? Nobody. The most learned man that ever lived, has no more actual knowledge of it than the most illiterate; and yet, when an honest and candid person questions the fact of its existence, he is regarded as very foolish, and as not a little wicked, withal; — while he who is obstreperously confident of its existence, and makes the assertion with the most dogmatic assurance, is thought to be possessed of great erudition and eminent virtue. Strange test of knowledge and goodness — yet how common!

The "next world!" For thousands of years have dreamers transmitted to their own and succeeding generations, the task of meditating upon a future existence, and still the whole subject is involved in impenetrable darkness. Man, unfortunately for himself, through the influence of erroneous teaching, wishes to exceed the limits of his sphere, and to transport himself beyond the visible world; he neglects experience, and feeds himself with conjectures. Early prepossessed against reason, he neglects its cultivation. Pretending to know his fate in another world, he is inattentive to his happiness in the present. We torment our lives by an insatiable desire of knowing and comprehending an imaginary state of existence, and perceive not the simple realities that comprise the extent of all possible knowledge. Could we be satisfied with facts and realities, and taking one world at a time, endeavor to make it what it should be, superseding Faith and Bigotry with Reason and Humanity, we should fit mankind to live properly *here;* and when this life is done they are properly prepared to live *hereafter* — admitting there is any.

WHAT WILL YOU SUBSTITUTE FOR RELIGION?

It is said by those, who, having been driven to their last stronghold in the cause of religion, and who, finding it no longer tenable upon its own intrinsic merits, are about to abandon its defence, that it would be better, infinitely better, not to remove this long-sanctioned curb upon the evil passions of mankind, even though there should be nothing real in it; that it would be vastly preferable not to demolish this ancient hedge round about the innocent and goodly disposed, even though it should be found to be but a baseless fabric, or, at best, founded upon mere inference.

Now it so happens, that in order to maintain this curb, so called, the perpetuation of ignorance, absolute ignorance, in the mass is indispensable. Light and knowledge threaten its utter destruction; for darkness, ignorance, and superstition are entirely unnecessary to the true happiness and wellbeing of man; and more and worse than that, they are extremely deleterious, except it be for the aggrandizement of a comparatively inconsiderable portion of the heritage. They must, they will be dispelled — it is contrary to the nature of things that they should forever exist.

But what shall be set up in the place of existing religion? has been asked.

Set nothing up as dogmatic and arbitrary, but cultivate a moral principle in the breast of man, without reference to, and totally independent of, any separate existence. Let him rely upon no superstruction that is not founded upon known facts. Instead of a long and incomprehensible creed, let his motto consist of these three words:

INJURE NO ONE. Whenever the question occurs with respect to the omission or commission of any act in the affairs of life, instead of referring for sanction to scripture, to the church, the ministry; to custom or fashion, let him ask himself the simple question, "Is the thing in itself right and proper to be done, or not done?" as the case may be; and as his best judgment shall dictate, so let him govern himself. This course would ensure salvation economically; and instead of man inheriting the costly necessity of redemption, it would be rendered needless to him, by his refraining from evil. It is impossible to calculate the amount of benefit to the family of man, in every point of view, were they to direct their united energies to these important points, instead of wasting them upon a system that will be found to be but as a broken reed, and a zeal for which, in many instances, has almost eaten them up. In his pecuniary resources, in this country alone, there would be a saving of millions of dollars annually, if man would abandon his servility to the church, and learn and follow the philosophy that is according to Nature and Reason.

INDIVIDUALITY.

Why should a man be afraid to be alone in his opinion? Somebody was once alone in about everything that is said, done, and believed in the world. One man, of all the millions, had in his great heart and measureless thought, the first seed of this whole order of things in which we live. A printing-press, a railroad, a steam engine, a plough, a system of education, moral reform, — Christianity itself is but the vibration of an individual force. There never was a giant but was a baby once; there is not a gigantic thing now, that was not once little. This very America, the sea-bed of all Anglo-Saxondom, into which it claims the right to flow and swallow everything else, was once, practically, as it were, in the head of a Genoese navigator, and it was not without headaching and severe throbs that it was ever got out.

It is not without trial and long toil, that a unit can swell itself to a host, that one long desire, finding words on one solitary tongue, can gather force enough to shake the nations; but as surely as it is great and true, it will be heard thrilling down to remotest time. Do you know that a thought, if true, is of import to the world? What if you, only, are its possessor?

That one thought shall be the centre of an ever-widening power, whose larger circles shall embrace, first you, then yours, and the world and worlds in their growing rings. Doubtless it requires courage and faith to be the announcer of a new truth which is to whelm old systems of oppression and falsehood in wide ruin, and beat hope out of a thousand blind hearts in the waste of their cherished error; but let us remember that a holier hope shall be wafted to a million hearts now hopeless, and the pained thousand shall be blessed as well as these.

How can the man be other than heroic, who feels within him the throes of a universal good, eager to be born of his kingly mind, who knows that the thought now throbbing in his brain may yet fill empires, years, and ages, with its blessed benediction? What are racks and inquisitions to him? What the poor wooden stocks of public opinion, or the hour's penance in the petty pillory of a little people's scorn? He makes his very outlawry his servant; the prison, to which mad parties doom him, shuts him out from babble and in with conscience and his own mind, and the pillory of hate and scorn becomes a pulpit under his feet, from which to reach the ears of thousands who had else not heard him. Valiant hearts have gone dead or mad, for the want of just such a field as the world opens now to the heroic, a field for intense action, calm-browed daring, and a bloodless victory. One eager for renown could ask no prouder laurels than wave in the path of reform. But the disciple of Truth has a higher arm than Fame's to rest his calm faith on; he feels the love of Right to be its own reward.

Only give a man a heart full of some good work, and he is not long in forgetting that he is alone in it, and learns readily that bugbears are the smallest of bears, that scarecrows will not scare MEN, and that hisses and hate, and gibbets even, are transient and petty things when seen in the light of an everlasting Truth. He can very cheaply dare to be hated by all earth's bigotry, who puts all earth's clear-eyed esteem in debt to him, and makes the whole future the rich banker of his fame. A few shallow years hiss round his quiet steps, and whole cycles chant melodious hymns to his high praise, after all reptile scorn has gone dead and dumb forever. The bold truth he spoke from lone corners to a few dull ears, begins to echo million-voiced from all the nations made glad in its power, and the smiles of joy, the deepened sense of life and good, the immeasurable delights of heart and mind, all grown from that accumulating thought, are the sweet notes that make the high psalm of his praise.

It matters not to the world-helper whether his name lives in the memory of those he has blessed, or dies with his body. If he remembers what was done, sees what is doing, and delights in the joy of earth, he is filled already; and if he does not pierce the veil, what matters to him the echo of a name he never hears? But Truth and Right do not defer their gifts. The *doing* good is the *having*. One shall not need to look to his neighbor, to the future, or the promises of the past, to find a price for his truthfulness. The flower asks no reward for shedding odors on the thankless air,—nay, does not even question if the sweet breath is needed; but, from a full and blushing heart, pours out the warm delight without measure, careless of recompense or fellowship. So, from the depth of a large humanity, the brother of suffering men breathes an unceasing soul of goodness round him, so that all hungry hearts may feed upon his kindness, and all benighted minds drink light into their opening eyes from that free-pouring and exhaustless fountain.

FREEDOM OF THE PRESS.

The incorrect definition of words is the cause of many errors, and of almost all disputes. The words *free press*, one would at first suppose meant a press open to the free discussion of all subjects on religion, morals, politics, and physics. But where is such a press to be found? Hardly in our country, the foundation of whose political institutions ought to be freedom and equality. All presses that have yet been called free are trammelled by two kinds of restrictions: law, and the prejudices of public opinion in favor of certain religious dogmas, party politics, etc.

In a country where the publishing of truth is considered a libel, and punished as such, the press cannot be called free; or when publishing anything contrary to the dogmas of any species of religion is a crime, punishable by fine and imprisonment, the word *free*, applied to the press, is certainly a misnomer. In all nations, any one may publish in favor of the ruling politics or religion, but in few is any one tolerated to publish anything against them; he is either physically punished by law, or morally injured by the persecution of those who, differing in opinion from him, assume the right of slandering and calumniating him for opinion's sake.

Complete toleration, physical and moral, exists nowhere; and often where the physical restrictions are most rigorous, the moral are most tolerant. Almost all the presses in our mercantile towns are hired and paid by the advertisements to advocate the monied and merchantile aristocracy; free and open to everything in favor of their supporters, and shut against every species of reasoning, be it ever so true, that can militate against them. All such presses cannot pretend to be called free. All political party, and all sectarian religious, presses are excluded from the list of free presses. Why boast of the free press of the United States, when there is not one in a hundred that has the least pretensions to the honorable title?

Would it not be better, and save much error and deception, to call everything by its proper name, that would designate its properties? For instance, this press is supported by the monied and mercantile aristocracies, to advocate their interests; that press is in favor of the government of the few over the many; one is in favor of the election of one man for President, and some of another; one is in favor of one religious sect, and some of another. Let us not permit the shop that deals only in whiskey, to pretend to sell bread.

DIFFERENCES OF OPINION.

An argument, be it good or bad, addresses itself never to the will, but always to the understanding. Whatever be the obstacles it has to combat, it acts by its own intrinsic force alone; and that is extraneous to our volition, and not controllable by it. But as a man's conduct, in this preliminary respect, can only be known accurately to himself, all laws for the punishment of opinions are acts of injustice and cruelty. All blame thrown upon a man, because his opinions are different from our own, is unjust. He has formed his opinion on such evidence as occurred to him, and we have done the same.

This view of the subject leads to charitable conclusions, to mutual forbearance and toleration. We are all in search of truth. It is never desirable to be misled or mistaken. If we are in error, and our neighbor has discovered the truth, it is the necessary result of his having enjoyed better means and opportunities, natural or acquired, than we have. Ought this to be a cause of anger and animosity against us? Our want of knowledge is a misfortune, not a crime, and charity should so consider it, provided always we do not conjoin bad passions and intolerant behavior to erroneous opinions.

As volition relates to actions only, and not to opinions, it follows that praise or blame, merit or demerit, reward or punishment, should be applied to actions only, and not to opinions. Punishment may produce resentment and hardness of heart, but it can never convince. Are we allowed to confute our adversary by replying to the major of his syllogism by a blow on the head; to his minor by imprisoning his person; or to his conclusion by setting the populace against him, as if he were a mad dog, unworthy of all argument? Yet, how often has this been done! Nay, at this very day, how common is the practice! And how much more common would it be, if public opinion did not show strong symptoms of dislike to persecution, whether for political errors, or theological heresies.

REFLECTIONS.

Choice by no means proves liberty, since hesitation only finishes when the will is determined by sufficient motives, and man cannot hinder motives from acting upon the will. The motive which determines the will is always the most powerful.

A little reflection will suffice to convince us that man is necessitated in all his actions. His ideas, opinions, and notions, true or false, are necessary fruits of his education; his passions and desires are necessary consequences of his natural temperament, and of the ideas with which he has been inspired. During his whole life, his volitions and actions are determined by his connections, habits, business, pleasures, conversations, and the thoughts that are involuntarily presented to his mind. He can desire and will, only what he judges advantageous or pleasing to himself; he is necessitated to choose what he judges most useful and agreeable.

When we trace the true principles of our actions, we find that they are always necessary consequences of our volitions and desires, which are never in our power. If the wicked act necessarily according to the impulses of their evil natures, society, in punishing them, acts necessarily by the desire for safety and preservation.

Reward and punishment are to be considered as the motives which should be employed to procure the adoption or abandonment of any given line of conduct. The doctrine of necessity does not in the least diminish the disapprobation of vice.

MOTHERS — CHILDREN.

"Every nation that has become great has had a race of noble matrons. Roman mothers made Roman men."

There is an important truth contained in this short paragraph, and it may not be uninteresting to make it the subject of a few reflections. The place which children hold in society depends very essentially, no doubt, on the character and conduct of the mother. In this busy nation, a husband is commonly too much occupied in his own affairs, to devote his thoughts and time to any systematic course of discipline. The sum of duty, comprising manners, cleanliness, associates, time out of school, amusements, morals, religious impressions, example, precept, temper and gentleness, depends mainly on the mother. She commonly feels the weight of her responsibility, and is willing faithfully to acquit herself of it. But she deserves every possible encouragement from her husband. The husband too often thwarts her purposes by interposing his own contradictory views. If he thinks he can do any good by his better knowledge, the medium of influence is through the mother. If he can kindly convince her of some better mode, he will best promote the common welfare by that course, and can do no greater mischief than by laying down rules that imply the insignificance of her judgment. It should be remembered that the prominent blessing of civilized society as to human life, is that it has made woman the joint and equal partner in domestic interests. If parents desire to make their children feel contempt for the authority of both of them, the readiest way to do it is to dispute in their presence. Which of them is a child to obey?

The bringing up of children is a fearful responsibility. So great is it that many parents feel that if they were not involved in it, and could have foreknown what it is, they never would have assumed it. But this distrust and dissatisfaction are, in part, from their own errors. Have they ever seriously thought how this duty should be performed? What books have they read? With whom have they conversed? What have they learned as to the best means of promoting the true interests of their offspring? If they have done nothing to inform themselves, how can they be instructors to others? Not only are parents bound to know what is right, but they are bound to know how to use knowledge in a right manner. One rule to-day, and a discordant one to-morrow; harshness and severity at one time, and the most weak and injurious indulgence at another, are poor qualities for instructors. There must be in these matters, as in everything else, a best way. It may be found somewhere in, or extracted from, these principles. Children have as good a right to be happy as their seniors. Their happiness consists in having and doing what will make them intellectually capable, morally correct and amiable, and physically pure and strong. These ends will be obtained by a systematic regularity, mildly and kindly, but certainly, enforced. Love, respect, and obedience are its consequences. A child will soon learn what it can have and do, and what it cannot; and it will soon know that it cannot ask again for what has been on due consideration refused. The excellence of society has its root in infancy, and that excellence is confided to the care of mothers. Its seeds are planted in the cradle.

PHILOSOPHY AND RELIGION.

Philosophy depends on argument; religion, on credulity: the one rests on the uniform experience of things; the other, on their violation. Philosophy does not parley with the apprehensions of the timid; it does not press into its service denunciations of eternal vengeance; its professors are not supplied by revenues extorted from the prime necessaries of the people; it requires no statutes villanously foisted into the legal code, to protect its tenets from disquisition, for truth and freedom, not falsehood and tyranny, are its aim.

Love of truth never raised a persecution. Persecution springs from the ambitious desire to govern the opinions of others, and thus convert them to their interested uses. And a religious ambition is by far the worst, the most rancorous, the most hateful and unreasonable specimen of its kind that ever infested the world; it is a direct violation of the rights of conscience, an atrocious and infamous invasion of the rights of man. A man wishes to compel me to think as he does, in order that I may subserve his purpose, not regarding my right to express my opinions being the same as he has to express his own; his opinions must be established, mine not dared to be uttered.

LIFE A JOURNEY.

Young persons think that they can see for themselves, and that they need not to be told what others have seen. But let us reduce this to common sense. Suppose a person to be under the necessity of going from the place in which he has lived, and which is familiar to him, to a far distant place. Let it be supposed that the road he must travel is crossed by many roads, and that he is frequently to find himself at points where several roads are seen, either one of which, so far as he can discern, may be the right one. Will it be of use to him to have been told, before he departs, which of these many roads to take? Will it help him onward to his destination, when he is bewildered and unable to decide for himself, to find some one who can assure him of the right course?

Life is a journey. Every step we take in it, brings us to something new, something unexpected, and perhaps entirely different from that which was looked for and expected. Those who have gone through it before us, have left us their instructions in what manner it is to be undertaken and accomplished. They tell us of their own troubles and difficulties;—they warn us how to avoid the like in our own journey. Which is wisest, to listen to them, and weigh the worth of their warning, or to push on heedlessly, and take the consequences?

THE GREAT PURPOSE OF SOCIAL LIFE.

There are laws prescribed to the human family, as there certainly are to other parts of animated being; and in attempting to show man's relation to the material world, and his duty to himself, in rendering obedience to laws as they are disclosed in nature, we, of course, anticipate social duty to some extent. All those qualities which enable an individual to comprehend life as a whole, and to obtain for himself the greatest good throughout its duration, enable him also to perform social duty. The social condition of the people of this country might be placed, it would seem, on a foundation better adapted to promote human happiness, than it is, if it were rightly understood. Labor and action, to useful ends, whether with the head or the hands, or both, is alike honorable in all classes, and constitutes the most enduring pleasure which is known in this life.

Every person belongs to a neighborhood which is both local and social. Even those who have removed into new countries, and who dwell in solitary abodes, do not lose the sentiment of neighborhood. The nearest person to them is a neighbor, though separated by long distance; and when this sentiment cannot be preserved in fact, it may be in thought, and by that means it usually is so. Perhaps the last impressions that depart from the mind of one who has wandered into far distant regions, are those made in his early days, in his native home. In general, as every one lives in a neighborhood more or less dense, he can promote his own happiness, and that of those around him, by observing a becoming moral conduct. He has a right to enjoy life, and to use all things which he has to that end; but he has not a right to any employment which necessarily disturbs that of others. Peace, tranquillity, and security within one's walls, is the main purpose of life. No one has a right to interfere in these things. The moral duties of neighborhood extend to all matters which minister to the common comfort, convenience, and security.

Every person, in general, is a member of some sort of society or association. These are intended for a useful purpose. Every one who is such a member has some duties to perform. He owes some proper part of his time, some proper contributions to the common object, and has an interest in the prosperity of the design. These institutions do some good, and some of them eminent good, in helping on the great purpose of social life, which is general improvement. Of this nature are public charities, lyceums, debating societies, libraries, reading-rooms, agricultural societies, and those for suppressing intemperance and immorality. No well-disposed citizen can conscientiously abstain from giving his aid and support to such objects. It is each one's duty to try to leave the world a little better than he found it. No one can say that these are matters which do not concern him. Suppose every one should say so, and had said so, from time immemorial, society would still be made up of barbarians. Every good that is done in any community affects, directly or indirectly, every member of it. The law of example, of imitation, of doing as others do, has a most pervading and astonishing influence. Every community is like a full vessel of water; no one drop in it can be moved without affecting every other drop.

NATURE AND REASON.

These are the only true teachers, and in proportion as we obey them we discover the folly of neglecting those things which concern human life, and involving ourselves in difficulties about questions that are but mere notions. Fancies beyond the reach of the understanding, and which have yet been made the object of belief — these have been the source of all the disputes, errors, and superstitions that have prevailed in the world. Such notional mysteries cannot be made subservient to the right uses of humanity.

PURPOSES OF LIFE.

We believe that human life rightly understood and rightly used is a beneficent gift, and that it can be so understood and used. It is irreconcilable to reason that man comes into this world only to suffer and mourn; it is from his own ignorance, folly, or error that he does so, whatever is said to the contrary. He is capable of informing himself; the means of doing this are within his power. If he were truly informed, he would not have to weep over his follies and errors. It is not pretended that every one can escape at once, from a benighted condition, and break into the region of reason and good sense. But it is most clear from what is well known to have happened in the world, that each generation may improve upon the preceding one, and that each individual in every successive period of time, may better know the true path, from perceiving how others have gone before him.

There can be no miracle in this. It will, at best, be a slow progress, and the wisdom arrived at in one age must command the respect of succeeding ones, and receive from them the melioration which they can contribute. We understand nothing of what is called the perfectibility of human nature; but we understand this, that if human nature can be made to know wherein its greatest good consists, it may be presumed that this good will be sought and obtained. Man was formed on this principle, and he acts on this principle, although he is seen so frequently to make the most deplorable and distressing mistakes. If it be not admitted that mankind will always strive to obtain whatsoever seems to them good, and strive to avoid whatsoever seems to them evil, then of course their moral teaching is in vain. If this principle be admitted, the sole inquiry is, what is good and what is evil.

PUNISHMENT.

Several benevolent and enlightened authors have endeavored to explain the use of penal laws, and to correct the ideas which formerly prevailed concerning public justice. Punishment is no longer considered, except by the ignorant and sanguinary, as vengeance from the injured, or expiation from the guilty. We now distinctly understand that the greatest possible happiness of the whole society must be the ultimate object of all just legislation; that the partial evil of punishment is consequently to be tolerated by the wise and humane legislator, only so far as it is proved necessary for the general good. When a crime has been committed, it cannot be undone by all the art or all the power of man; by vengeance the most sanguinary, or remorse the most painful.

The past is irrevocable; all that remains is to provide for the future. It would be absurd, after an offence has already been committed, to increase the sum of misery in the world by inflicting pain upon the offender, unless that pain were afterwards to be productive of good to society, either by preventing the criminal from repeating his offence or by deterring others from similar enormities. With this double view of restraining individuals, by the recollection of past sufferings, from future crimes, and of teaching others by public example, to expect and fear certain evils as the necessary consequences of certain actions hurtful to society, all wise laws are framed and all just punishments inflicted. It is only by the conviction that certain punishments are essential to the general security and happiness, that a person of humanity can or ought to fortify his mind against the natural feelings of compassion.

These feelings are the most painful and the most difficult to resist, when, as it sometimes unavoidably happens, public justice requires the total sacrifice of the happiness, liberty, and perhaps the life, of a fellow-creature, whose ignorance precluded him from virtue, and whose neglected or depraved education prepared him, by inevitable degrees, for vice and all its miseries. How exquisitely painful must be the feelings of a humane judge, in pronouncing sentence upon such an unfortunate being! But the law permits of no refined metaphysical disquisitions. It would be vain to plead the necessitarian's doctrine of an unavoidable connection between the past and the future, in all human actions, or perhaps it would be more proper to say, that the doctrine of necessity obtains here, as elsewhere; for the same necessity compels the punishment that compels the crime.

RIGHT DOCTRINE.

No man should be delicate about asking for what is properly due him. If he neglects doing so, he is deficient in the spirit of independence which he should observe in all his actions. Rights, if not granted, should be demanded. The selfish world is little inclined to give one his own, unless he has the manliness to claim it.

LEARNING A TRADE.

There are many people who dislike the name of mechanic, and who would, rather than put their children to an honest trade, tug hard at their business and live sparingly, for the purpose of giving them a college education. They think meanly of him who wears a leather apron and is not dressed in the latest fashion. This we believe is the reason why there are so many pettifoggers and vagabonds in the world. Many a son has been sent to college with the expectation of his parents highly excited, but like the fable of the mountain, he produced only a mouse. We think highly of our colleges and literary institutions, and rejoice to see them prosper, but we are more pleased to see an individual's mind turned in a right current. There are hundreds of lawyers who would have made better mechanics and have obtained a more comfortable livelihood. And we have no doubt that there are many mechanics who would stand high at the bar, had they been blessed with a liberal education. But if a child have talents they will not remain hid, and no matter what his trade or profession is, they will sooner or later burst forth. There are many distinguished individuals in the literary world who were bred to mechanical trades. Many of the editors of our best-conducted journals were mechanics, and do credit to the station they occupy. And our mechanics too, generally speaking, are the most industrious part of the community. They are almost always busily employed. But it is apt to be otherwise with professional men. They are often idle, lazy. It is an effort for them to bend their minds to a difficult pursuit. They are well informed, because they spend much of their time in reading: but this is an unprofitable business unless we have some definite object in view.

In these remarks we wish it not to be understood that we think lightly of professional men generally, for we do not. We wish to address ourselves particularly to those parents who are hesitating what occupations to give their children. Are they ingenious, fond of mechanical pursuits? Give them a trade. Do they love to study, and cannot give their attention to anything else? Send them to college. Let your children choose themselves what trade or profession they will follow, and what they select will generally prove the most advantageous in the end. But never think a trade too humble for your son to work at, nor a profession too important for him to acquire. Let every parent pursue this course with his children, and we are confident there would be less unhappiness and misery in the world. You can never force a trade or profession upon a child; it must be natural to him. A disregard of a child's inclination in this respect, has often proved his ruin, or at least unfitted him for the duties of life.

HOME CONVERSATION.

Children hunger perpetually for new ideas, and the most pleasant way of reception is by the voice and ear, not by the eye and the printed page.

The one mode is natural, the other artificial. Who would not rather listen than read? We not unfrequently pass by in the papers a full report of a lecture, and then go and pay our money to hear the selfsame words uttered. An audience will listen closely from the beginning to the end of an address, which not one in twenty of those present would read with the same attention. This is emphatically true of children. They will learn with pleasure from the lips of parents what they deem it drudgery to study in the books; and even if they have the misfortune to be deprived of the educational advantages which they desire, they cannot fail to grow up intelligent if they enjoy in childhood and youth the privilege of listening daily to the conversation of intelligent people. Let parents, then, talk much and talk well at home. A father who is habitually silent in his own house, may be, in many respects, a wise man, but he is not wise in his silence.

We sometimes see parents, who are the life of every company which they enter, dull, silent, uninteresting at home among their children. If they have not mental activity and mental stores sufficient for both, let them first provide for their own household. It is better to instruct children and make them happy at home, than it is to charm strangers or amuse friends. A silent house is a dull place for young people, a place from which they will escape if they can. The youth who does not love home is in danger. Make home, then, a cheerful and pleasant spot. Light it up with cheerful, instructive conversation. Father, mother, talk your best at home.

IMPROVEMENT OF MANKIND.

To attempt to improve mankind on any other principle than by a close, accurate, and undeviating attention to facts, is as absurd and unavailing as to expect that man, immersed in ignorance, and surrounded by every vicious temptation, shall be better, wiser, and happier than when trained to be intelligent and active, amid circumstances only which would perpetually unite his interest, his duty, and his feelings. The state of the world will never be materially improved until knowledge shall be more generally diffused, and the multitude are taught to act from a just sense of their own interest, rather than from passion and prejudice. Hitherto, mankind have scarcely come to the investigation of the condition of their being, with half of their reasoning powers; the residue have been absorbed by a legitimatized superstition, begotten in youth on their ignorance, matured by precept and example, and confirmed by surrounding bigotry.

The ideas of men are acquired, and these ideas are enlarged, corrected, and strengthened by intelligent intercourse; they can advance only by degrees — can attain to no state of knowledge but by a progression more or less slow. After many defective attempts, they are enabled to distinguish, by comparison, that which is well or ill of every kind; so that what is called an art, is but the result of reason and experience reduced to a method. Whatever savors of religious superstition, either in the arts or in speculative science, can only subserve the purpose of their restriction, and impede their course and their progress. The reason why the sciences have not advanced more is, that scholars have been afraid to depart from the ideas entertained by the schools, lest they should sacrifice their prospects, or draw down upon them the ire of old-fashioned professors; and if a man dare advance a sentiment with respect to morals or religion at variance with doctrine whipped into his grandfather a hundred and fifty years ago, it is immediately said: "He is wise above what is written," and he is represented as that terrible monster — an infidel.

While authority, prejudice, and power have pertinaciously contended that it was necessary to restrict freedom of inquiry; that there might be too much boldness of opinion, and too much liberty of intellectual enterprise — the strong necessities and genuine interests of mankind have slowly but steadily urged them onward to an indefinite perception of their rights, and a corresponding assertion of claims to the natural exercise of their privileges. It is much to be lamented that too many people even yet conceive that there are some opinions which ought not to be tolerated, as they imagine that the free expression of them would tend to disorganize society, by subverting what they believe to be the foundation of virtue. How can any danger possibly arise from the unrestrained expression of any opinion whatever, where reason and truth are left free to combat them? It is time the world had done with such groundless apprehensions: they have been sources of infinite mischief in all ages and in every country. Such people appear to breathe the very spirit of despotism, and act as if they wish to communicate it. It is impossible not to infer from their apprehensions, that as men increase in knowledge they must see reason to disapprove the systems established. How can that mind be constituted which contemplates the progress of human knowledge as matter of regret or fear? The wider the diffusion of knowledge, the better the people are informed, the more they understand — the more likely they are to see and comprehend what is for their good, and the means by which that good is to be attained; the more likely they are to abstain from such means as would be prejudicial in their operation, and calculated rather for the prevention than the attainment of that good.

THIS WORLD.

We have often said that we thought it a waste of time and talent to anticipate our destiny beyond the grave, and to make preparations for an existence of which we know nothing, and for which, therefore, we cannot prepare. Yet it is an excellent thing to look before us, and to be provident, if we will not look too far. He who takes thought for the present moment only, is hardly entitled to the character of a rational, reflecting being.

The concerns of eternity have swallowed up much time and money, and the great concerns of time have been often neglected. There is one important subject, whose investigation might probably occupy, with advantage to mankind, the thoughts and the talents that are now bestowed upon worlds beyond the stars. It is this:—

The civilized world in modern days, has been enriched by very wonderful investigations. Its powers of production have increased in an astonishing manner. It has thus acquired the capability of supplying all its wants with much less labor than formerly; and if that capability were alone necessary in order to produce happiness and comfort, the modern civilized world would be most marvellously happy and comfortable. It is the very reverse. Almost in proportion as men have learned to produce easily, has the reward of their exertions been lessened; and at the present hour, machines to save labor are found to cause starvation to the laborer; for the markets are glutted, and employment fails. Now, instead of studying what men tell us are oracles delivered to our forefathers some thousand years ago by spirits of the air, and instead of imagining what may happen to us after sensation appears extinct — instead, we say, of these supernatural speculations, were it not better that we examine and solve, if we can, the following question:

Is there any remedy for the frightful evils of national abundance?

A FUTURE LIFE.

The great majority of mankind think that a belief in future existence is absolutely necessary to present happiness. We believe the doctrine to be a mistake. Time a thousand years hence is no more to us now, than time a thousand years past. As no event could have harmed us when we existed not, so no event can possibly harm us when we are no more. By anticipating and calculating too much on future felicity, and dreading, or at least fearing, future misery, man often loses sight of present enjoyments and neglects present duties. When men shall discover that nothing can be known beyond this life, and that there is no rational ground for any such belief, they will begin to think more of improving the condition of the human species. Their whole thoughts will then be turned upon what man has done, and what he can still do, for the benefit of man. As they will be delivered from all fear of invisible voluntary agents, that may do them harm, so they will no longer look up to such agents for help, but they will study more their own powers and the powers and properties of Nature. They will discover how much time and labor are spent entirely uselessly, and worse than uselessly — perniciously; that so far from improving the condition of man, such labors only tend to destroy his own peace, and render him an enemy to his fellow-man.

THE INFLUENCE OF WOMAN.

From the cradle to the grave of man, woman exercises an all-pervading and unintermitted influence upon his character and destiny. She calls forth and directs his earliest knowledge. All that is good in him, all that is true, is owing to her watchful and tireless nurture of his instincts. In the helplessness of infancy woman is to him a Providence, awakening in him those feelings, which afterwards rise and expand to philanthropy and virtue. She is his earliest conception of perfect goodness. Through the whole of his mortal existence, a mother's love is to him a bright and visible symbol of absolute excellence, — pure, unselfish, self-sacrificing, unchanging, unquenchable; it goes out with him in all the alternations of life, — in sorrow and in joy, in sickness and health, — rejoicing and sorrowing with him and for him and for him alone; clinging to him with a closer grasp when all have deserted him, and because all have deserted him, and even in disgrace and infamy not forsaking him, — love stronger than pain, than death and the grave.

The dreams of the young man are of paradise; a garden heaven-environed, fanned by wings of angels, in which ever bloom flowers of celestial fragrance, in whose walks he hears the soft voices of unseen spirits. Yet the garden is without beauty, the voices utter no music unless there be an Eve to listen with him, and to wander with him among the groves of the garden. In this period of the poetry of his existence, woman, either for good or evil, is nearly all in all, the cynosure of his thoughts and feelings. When he descends into the prose regions of the business and matter-of-fact of life, he still finds himself under a moral necessity of taking woman as his companion and aid. He finds the walks of business empty, the crowded mart a desert, unless around their precincts hover visions of beloved forms at home, which light up the desert and the solitude with smiles. In every period of his life it has been true, that: —

> "The world was sad, the garden was a wild,
> And man, the hermit, sighed, till woman smiled."

Undoubtedly, the dreams of the youth, and the calculations of the man, are often destined to woful and disastrous disappointment. The poetry, when committed to paper, too often comes out without rhyme or reason, intolerable blank verse, or miserable, halting doggerel. The prose, too, is unreadable, full of uncouth idioms and false syntax. Eve, after all, often proves herself a mere mortal, and that not of the highest cast. The angel is sometimes a spirit of another sort than one of light. The companion is occasionally one, with whom a quiet man would be loth to associate forever. But still, in every circumstance, woman affects, with good or bad influences, the condition and character of man through the whole of life.

It is a truth, universally assumed and admitted, that there is no test of the advancement of civilization so sure and infallible, as that afforded by the position of woman in society, the rank assigned to her in the scale of social adjustment. It is a just and true test; for civilization, in its ultimate analysis, is the overthrow of the law of force. Wherever the law of force, the right of the strongest, prevails, woman must be, by the physical laws of nature, inferior and degraded. As this law recedes, woman will be exalted, and the degree of her elevation will be the index of the degree in which the law of force has yielded to the law of right. The influence of woman is a purely moral influence. Her physical constitution and intellectual temperament debar her from any other. Her place in society may, therefore, be taken as a fair indication of the relative predominance of right and force.

OLD AGE.

When the summer of youth is slowly wasting away into the nightfall of age, and the shadows of the past year grow deeper and deeper, and life wears to its close, it is pleasant to look back through the vista of time, upon the sorrows and felicities of our earlier years. If we have a home to shelter, and hearts to rejoice with us, and friends have been gathered together around our fireside, then the rough places of our wayfaring will have been worn and smoothed away in the twilight of life, while the sunny spots we have passed through will grow brighter and more beautiful. Happy, indeed, are they whose intercourse with the world has not changed the tone of holier feeling, or broken those musical chords of the heart, whose vibrations are so melodious, so tender and touching in the evening of age.

LIGHT AND DARKNESS.

Two great movements at the present time stand arrayed in irreconcilable hostility. The one tends onward to the elevation of humanity in the age of universal wisdom; the other, backward to primeval darkness, superstition, moral corruption, despotism, and the eternal stagnation of thought. From the irrepressible energies of the human intellect, still struggling for additional truth, and the continual struggle of the indwelling moral sense against the wrongs and miseries of human life, necessarily arises the party of progress, protesting against despotism, falsehood and inhumanity, while introducing new science, new philosophy and new forms of social organization for human welfare.

The lower forms of human development, the animalized men whose perverted intellect cherishes self-evident falsehoods, and whose moral sense is not disturbed by wrongs and outrages, nor by the sight of constant suffering and degradation, who cannot realize the genuine nature of man, or believe in the possibility of any higher condition of society than that which has existed, are necessarily the antagonists of every movement which seeks to realize a far higher condition of knowledge and happiness. The result of the struggle between these opposing powers cannot be doubtful, although it may be tedious; for notwithstanding that in ancient times all power was in the hands of the despotic party, freedom has now sufficient footing on the earth, and a sufficiently secure lodgement in the bosoms of mankind to insure her triumph.

But the most formidable difficulty in the way of such a triumph arises from the fact that the legions of despotism are fully aware of the doom which must overtake them whenever the human mind is left free in the acquisition of knowledge, fully aware that their power is based upon delusion and superstitious impressions, and that their system can be perpetuated only by perverting the intellect of the young. Here, then, is the struggle. Shall the young be free in their education, or shall they be made the victims of the power which their parents and teachers may tyrannically use? In this form is the question now brought before us by that terrible power which sits enthroned at Rome, which claims the allegiance of the entire world, which demands a spiritual, legal, and military supremacy over all forms of government, whether democratic or monarchical, and which, in short, aspires to and demands the dominion of the world. A power, which, with all its Jesuitical craft and pliant adaptation to the humors of mankind, has not even thought it necessary to veil its real purpose, or to deny its despotic pretensions. Its bishops and priests and editors make no secret of the claims of Romanism to overrule all forms of government, and to suppress by military power all other forms of religion, whenever that power can be obtained.

The leading Roman Catholic editors of France, England, and the United States, under the sanction of the Roman Catholic bishops, boldly avow that religious toleration is utterly incompatible with Romanism, and that their church is of necessity intolerant, that Roman Catholics who make any profession of liberality or toleration, are doing violence to the doctrines of their church and uttering what they should know to be untrue. And while Romanists loudly demand toleration and freedom for the oppressed Roman Catholics of Ireland, they as loudly insist upon maintaining religious and political despotism wherever Romanism controls the military power. Whoever is faithful to Rome and assists by bayonet and ball in crushing Italian liberty, and keeping down the democracy of Europe by means of prisons, chains and gibbets, is honored by the pope and the entire Roman Catholic Church throughout the world, even though his life be notoriously black with all the infamy which belongs to a penitentiary convict. To enslave mankind by means of cunning priestcraft, by the halter, the lash, and the dungeon, the spy and the assassin, is the aim of Rome, and in accomplishing her purpose she welcomes the co-operation of every despot, knave, and military robber.

To assert that any thorough Romanist can be a Republican, a friend of toleration, a friend of human progress in thought and liberty, or can be anything else than a steady supporter of political and mental despotism, is to contradict the universal history of that Church, the declarations of its high authorities, and the admissions which its very apologists and advocates have made, under the strongest temptation to conceal and deny its true character.

It is therefore pre-eminently the duty of those who belong to the advance-guard of human progress, who are struggling for reforms which society is not yet prepared to grant, and for a philosophy which the present century can scarcely adopt, to arouse themselves against the most formidable enemy that reform has ever had to contend with. Wherever Romanism extends its jurisdiction, there is an end to reform, to liberty, and to liberal philosophy, which Romanism knows to be incompatible with its own existence. The best of modern literature is proscribed by Rome, and the practice of phrenology and other sciences prohibited by the same authority.

Let us not forget, in the midst of our liberty and security, that a power which has come down as a black cloud from the dark ages, still the same infallible, unchangeable body, — still the open ally and the principal supporter of despotism, — still the same adversary of science as in the days of Galileo, is here in our midst, with a discipline, unity, fanaticism, and ignorance in its masses; cunning in its leaders, and wealth and foreign support, possessed by no other organization, and so conscious of its strength, as to throw off its disguise and confess its despotic aims.

PRIDE.

There is a kind of pride which is often mistaken for self-respect. We hear of honorable and of laudable pride. We take pride to be that self-esteem in which a man holds himself. It may be founded in his estimation of the qualities of his mind, in his attainments, in his possessions, in his strength, his beauty, his parentage, or descent. It may also be founded in a consciousness of virtue, and of having faithfully done one's duty in all the relations of life. It seems to arise necessarily, from comparing one's self with other persons. If this be the right meaning of pride, it is very clear that it is not always a sentiment which entitles one to respect himself. A man would be thought to be very unwise, who should openly declare that he valued himself, in comparison with other men, on account of his wealth, his beauty, or his family connection; equally unwise if he should declare his opinion of himself to be, that he was superior to other men in the gift of natural intellect, in the cultivation of it, or in the practice of the various virtues.

The common sense of mankind, founded on natural reason, does not approve of that self-gratulation which rests upon the accident of birth, of inheritance, nor even upon the acquisition of fortune by one's own industry; nor does it approve of that feeling, when founded upon qualities which belong to the mind, nor even in the practice of the virtues, unless when manifested in a certain manner.

There must be, in the very nature of things, some persons in every community, large or small, who are superior to others in these sources of self-esteem. In every city, town, and village in this nation, there are some persons who are in possession of some of these causes of self-esteem in some comparative degree, and other persons who have the fewest or the least of them. Those who so use their advantages as to entitle themselves to the esteem of others, and who are acknowledged to be respectable for that use, may well be entitled to respect themselves from such causes. Those who use them in such a manner as to announce the feeling of superiority over others, and habitually to offend the watchful feeling of self-love, are very properly called *the proud.* It is believed that these views conform to natural law, and to the necessary constitution of human society.

LIVING AND DYING.

There are some persons who see, in the order of succession inherent in animal and vegetable creation, that the system is defective, and does not satisfy "the longings of the immortal soul." They complain of the principle of decay; of the yellow leaf of autumn; of the dreariness of winter. They complain more of the uncertainty, and sometimes sudden termination, of human life; that the young and the serviceable die; that death, at any age, is a mournful and afflictive event. They say that this world is "a vale of tears," that "man is born to trouble, as the sparks fly upward," that our "days are few, and full of trouble," and that there is no happiness but in heaven, or in another state of existence. This is not what Nature says. This is the language of ignorant, erring, ungrateful man. There is no one thing which declares the wisdom and the goodness of Nature more convincingly, than the provision for the commencement, the duration, and the end of life. Whatsoever there may seem to be of evil in it, is either of man's own creating, or it is because he does not or will not exercise his reason. If it were left to man to regulate this matter, what would he please to do? Would he make everything that comes into being, as vegetable, continue in it, and for how long a time? What would become of the succession of blossoms and fruits? Would he make his own race immortal on the earth? What would he do with the pleasures and duties of youth, manhood, decline and old age? Would he continue all in life, who come into it, indefinitely? How would or could any being come into life, if the laws of Nature were deranged? If it were possible to suppose that all to whom life is given, were to remain on earth and continue to multiply, what would life come to be?

It better becomes complaining mortals to be assured that Nature acts wiser than they. It is their proper duty to exercise the beneficent gift of reason to learn that it is so; that death proceeds no less from the goodness of Nature, than birth; that man abuses or perverts the beautiful order of succession, as he does everything else, when ignorant and disobedient. If he used his faculties in accordance with reason, he would know that from this order arise all the relations which call forth the highest moral perfection to which he can aspire, all incitements to virtue, all the promptings to self-satisfying actions, and all the delights of an intelligent, philosophic mind.

INTELLECTUAL PLEASURES.

Placed as mankind are in a world filled with beautiful and interesting objects, and possessing faculties which find their exercise and enjoyment in the contemplation of these objects, it becomes them to investigate their nature, in other words, to pursue knowledge. Surely it is impossible for a reasonable man to avoid this conclusion, that by cultivating the powers with which he is endowed, and employing them on objects within his reach, he is not only consulting his own happiness, but rendering himself useful to his fellowmen.

The variety and intensity of intellectual pleasures must in a great degree depend on the number of truths with which the individual may be acquainted, for by such means only, combined with reflection, the consequence of knowledge, can the powers of judgment be improved. Now, all men, whose organization is not unusually imperfect, are capable of acquiring knowledge to an extent of which, from our present inconsistent system of education, we can form but an inadequate idea. What is so well calculated to enlarge and fill the mind with admiration as astronomy? And yet, some of the truths in this science, once considered so abstruse and comprehended only by a Newton, are now within the reach of every capacity. When the minds of the great mass of mankind are no longer permitted to lie waste, but shall be properly cultivated, and under the genial influence of equitable institutions, a taste for intellectual enjoyments will become as general as the desire for bodily nutriment; and although the want of intelligence may be little felt by an ignorant individual, yet it is far more grievous than want of wealth. The man who is born blind, knows not his misery; so the man who is trained up in ignorance, thinks himself equal with him of superior intelligence; but there is as much difference in this respect between man and man, as between man and animal.

It is on this account that it is of so much importance in the education of youth to encourage their instinctive taste for the beauty and sublimity of Nature; while it opens to the young a source of pure and permanent enjoyment, it has consequences on the character and happiness of their coming lives which they are unable to foresee. It is to provide them, amid all the agitations and trials of society, with a gentle, unreproaching friend whose voice is ever in alliance with goodness and virtue, and which, when once understood, is able both to soothe misfortune and to reclaim from folly. It is to identify them with the happiness of that nature to which they belong, and to give them an interest in every species of being which surrounds them; and amid the hours of curiosity and delight, to awaken those latent feelings of benevolence and sympathy from which all the moral and intellectual greatness of man finally arises; it is a companion to him which no misfortune can repress, no clime destroy, no enemy alienate, no despotism enslave. It is at home a friend, abroad an introduction, in solitude a solace, in society an ornament; it chastens vice, it guides virtue, and it gives at once a grace and an ornament to genius.

Let a man but have a taste for books and the means of gratifying it, and he can hardly fail of being a happy man, unless indeed we place in his hands a most perverse selection. We place him in contact with the best society in every period of history, with the wisest, wittiest, the tenderest, the bravest, and the purest characters that have adorned humanity. We make him an inhabitant of all nations, a contemporary of all ages. It is hardly possible but the character should take a higher and better tone from the constant habit of associating in thought with a class of thinkers who, to say the least, are above the average of humanity. It is morally impossible but that the manners should take a tinge of good breeding and civilization from having constantly before one's eyes, the way in which the best bred and best informed men have talked and conducted themselves in their intercourse with each other. There is a gentle but perfectly irresistible coercion in a habit of reading, well directed, over the whole tenor of a man's character and conduct, which is not the less effectual because it is really the last thing he dreams of. It civilizes the conduct of men, and suffers them not to remain barbarous. A well-conducted system of education can hardly fail, also, of making an industrious man. Where the mind has been trained to activity, the body necessarily follows its incitements, while habits of sottishness will be deserted for more congenial intellectual exercises.

EVILS.

There are many evils which deform and disgrace society, and which do their full part in making this a world of evil. There is squalid, miserable poverty; there is disgusting, lamentable vice; there is horrible crime and public execution. All these things, it is said, are inevitable; they spring from the very nature of man, and from the laws which compel him to dwell in social connection. It is questionable whether there must be poverty; surely, there need not be vice and crime. The whole number of Quakers in the United States is many thousands. When did any one see a Quaker begging in the streets; or an intoxicated Quaker; or any one of this class of citizens, at the criminal bar? Are not these people engaged in the common affairs of the world; are not they merchants, mechanics, artificers, mariners, and otherwise employed in the ordinary business of life? They, like the rest of us, are subject to the temptations and perversions incident to our state of being. Here, then, is a clear demonstration, that even without the aid of civil power, but by the mere force of moral influence, there is a class of men, in the midst of society, who do escape disgraceful poverty, and who are free from vice and crime.

DUTY AND HAPPINESS.

The difficulty with religionists is this:— They try to make mankind believe that duty calls one way, while all the dictates of reason and common sense seem to teach their *interest*, that is, their *happiness*, requires them to take a different course; hence a conflict ensues between *duty* and happiness, and this is the reason why so many pursue the latter, and so few the former course.

It is time, therefore, high time, indeed, that these teachers should be brought to see that any course that does not lead to happiness, — happiness that is seen, — happiness that can be realized for a certainty, is not, and cannot be a duty; but if it does lead to happiness, then it is for one's own interest or profit to pursue it.

Let all our would-be reformers take this course. Say nothing about duty, or even moral, much less religious obligation; say nothing about God or his law, about which men have disputed so long, to no purpose. But let them point out the natural and philosophical consequences of all moral actions as far as they are known, or their consequences can be traced; and let them frame all their laws agreeably to these rules, and then leave mankind to think what they please, speak and write what they think, and do what they choose, so long as they transgress no law; but if they do, then let them abide the consequences of that, as they must of all other of their actions. No man will strive knowingly to promote his own misery; and therefore if he does it, it must be owing to ignorance, or some ungoverned passion, or both.

UNIVERSAL BENEVOLENCE.

Humanity has lessons full of salutary instruction, and calculated to enforce civilization upon the intellectual powers of man. The spiritualization of human existence has been an injury to man; it has taught him to spurn at matter, to contemn its power and ridicule its essence; whereas, on the contrary, sound philosophy, unfolding as it does the connection between man and Nature, is fitted to produce in the mind sentiments of respect and tranquillity; respect for the aggregate of existence to which he belongs, and tranquillity at the idea of an eternal interest (as a race) in this indestructible mass. The successive changes through which he is destined to pass, and the impossibility of relinquishing his connection with Nature, should inspire him with feelings of universal sympathy, and with sentiments of universal benevolence. Human reason has an important duty to perform in the institutions which it establishes; for these institutions will affect in succession all the portions of matter destined to pass through an organized condition.

It is, no doubt, difficult to convince the human understanding of this physical or universal connection, or to make man see his true interest in this respect. It is, nevertheless, a solemn and philosophic truth that our sensations are at this moment suffering under the cruel lash of ancient institutions; that the whole animal world are reciprocating with each other a system of extensive and perpetual wretchedness, resulting principally from that contempt which has been thrown upon the capacity of material substance, and our ignorance of an important and an indestructible connection with the great body of Nature. If man had a comprehensive view of the successive changes of his existence, and a correct idea of the nature of sensation continually resulting from the renovation of organic forms, sympathy or universal benevolence would become irresistibly impressive upon his moral powers and form the basis of his subsequent conduct.

This principle should also be extended to the whole universal world, so as to exclude acts of cruelty and annihilate every species of injustice. The child who is permitted in early life to run a pin through a fly, is already half prepared to run a dagger through the heart of his fellow-creature. It is the duty of parents and the business of instruction, to correct the ferocious errors of former ages, and inspire society with sentiments of sympathy and universal goodness. But to do this with effect, political institutions the world over must be changed and placed upon the broad basis of universal liberty and universal justice. This would be a work of time, but it is as certain in the ultimate issue of things, as the progress of the earth around the sun, or the general revolution of the planetary system. The individual who withholds his intellectual contribution in this respect, is either misinformed, or a traitor in the great cause of human existence.

TRUTH — TEACHINGS OF NATURE.

The discovery and the development of *Truth* as it really exists in the system of Nature, is of the highest importance to the true interests of mankind. But how to present this truth to the view of the mind in a manner calculated to attract its attention, is difficult for us to say. For although the uncorrupted faculties of man cannot be opposed to the attractive charms of truth, or the brilliant beauties of her native appearance, yet so numerous are the causes, and so powerful their operation, which serve to mislead the mind and produce injurious impressions upon it, that perspicuity and regularity of thought are essentially deranged, and the clearness of scientific deductions are swallowed up in the gulf of error and deception. This process, prejudicial to our mental operations, commences in the early part of our existence, and proceeds with a regularity of mischievous consequences, to the period when man assumes the dignity of intellectual independence; and fortunate indeed is that individual who arrives to this elevated condition of mental existence. The energy of thought, when applied to the discovery of truth, is naturally calculated to sweep away the rubbish of error, and cut up those deep-rooted prejudices which have so long retarded the useful improvement of our species. The grand object of philosophic philanthropists should be, to extend the sphere of mental energy, to enlarge the circle of its influence, and to oppose the persevering activity of mind to the fallen rancor of superstition and the destroying fury of fanaticism.

Religious enthusiasm, bigotry, and superstition, conjoined with the strong arm of political despotism, have rendered men, in the past ages of the world, the degraded instruments of their own pernicious and destructive purposes; it is here we must seek for the source of many human misfortunes, and the perpetuation of those prejudices by which the body and mind are both enslaved. It is true that the natural imbecility and imperfection of our faculties, and the extensive nature and variety of those moral and physical combinations from which science is to be deduced, evince the strong probability that man may frequently be erroneous in the conclusions which he draws from certain premises, because the force of his faculties is not adequate to a full and complete investigation of the compounded and diversified relations of our existence; but these natural obstacles to the clear deductions of science, are neither of a discouraging nor an insurmountable nature.

There is no system either of education, politics, or religion, which ought to be excepted from the severest scrutiny of the human mind, or the minutest examination which the human faculties can bestow upon it; yet habit and custom of long duration have so strongly attached man to his errors, that he reluctantly relinquishes those tenets which serve only to disturb his peace and destroy his happiness; while the privileged impostors of the world, or those who feast upon the continuation of error and prejudice, unite their strongest exertions to persuade man that his most important interests, in time and eternity, depend upon the preservation of ancient and unnatural establishments, which in fact, are as destructive to human felicity as they are derogatory to the divine purity of supreme intelligence.

That happiness is to be preferred to misery; pleasure, to pain; virtue, to vice; truth, to falsehood; science, to ignorance; order, to confusion; and universal good, to universal evil,— are positions that no rational being can possibly controvert. They are positions to which mankind, in all ages and countries, must yield assent. They are positions, the truth of which is never denied, the essence of which is never controverted; it is the form or application only which has been the cause of social contention, and not the reality or excellence of the axioms themselves.

The universality of the principle of sensation, generates universal capacity of enjoying pleasure, and suffering pain. This circumstance modifies the character of human actions, and renders it necessary that every man should regard every other man with an eye of strict justice, with a tender and delicate sensibility, with a constant reference to the preservation of his feelings, and the extension of his happiness; in a word, that the exercise of eternal justice should be constantly reciprocated by all the individuals of the same species. If we assume to ourselves the pretended right of injuring the sensations, the moral sentiments, or general happiness of our neighbors, they have, undoubtedly, an equal right to commit the same violence upon us; this would go to the destruction of all right, to the total subversion of all justice; it would reduce society instantly to a state of warfare, and introduce the reign of terror and misery.

It is a contradiction of terms to assert that any man has a right to do wrong; the exercise of such a pretended right is the absolute destruction of all right, and the first human being who commits this violation has already prepared for himself a hell of retaliation, the justice of which his own mind can never deny. It is, therefore, inconsistent with the truth to say that there is no such thing as a general standard of moral excellence; this standard has a real existence in the construction of human nature; it is ascertained and regulated by the rule of reciprocal justice.

PLEASURES.

Sensible pleasures, — or the gratification of the senses, are to be avoided when they tend to injure the corporal and mental faculties. They are to be avoided when they tend to the injury of our neighbors, or are calculated to produce in ourselves, habits of stratagem and deceit. Thus far all systems of morality and rational conduct are agreed. But the preachers of self-denial add to these limitations a prohibition to the frequent indulgence of sensible pleasures, from the danger of suffering ourselves to set too great a value on them, and to postpone the best and most elevated, to the meanest. Having assumed this new principle of limitation, there is no visionary and repulsive extreme to which these sectaries have not in some instances proceeded. They have regarded all sensible pleasures as a deduction from the purity and dignity of the mind, and they have not abstained from invective against intellectual pleasure itself. They have taught men to court persecution and calumny. They have delighted to plant thorns in the path of human life. They have represented sorrow, anguish, and mortification, as the ornaments and honor of our existence.

Now it is a mistake, we think, to suppose that sensible pleasures and intellectual ones are by any means incompatible. He that would have great energy, cannot perhaps do better than to busy himself in various directions, and to cultivate every part of his nature. Man is a little world, as it were, within himself, and every portion of that world is entitled to attention. A wise man wishes to have a sound body, as well as a sound mind. He would wish to be a man at all points. For this purpose he would exercise and strengthen the muscles of every part of his frame. He would prepare his body to endure hardship and vicissitude. He would exercise his digestive powers. He would cultivate the delicacy of the organs of taste. He would not neglect the proper and right use and enjoyment of all the faculties and functions of his being. There is a harmony and a sympathy through every part of the human machine. A vigorous and animated tone of body contributes largely to the advantage of the intellect, and an improved state of intellect heightens and refines our sensible pleasures. A modern metaphysician, of great reputation in the religious world, has maintained life to be an unnatural state, and death the genuine condition of man. If this thesis is to be admitted, it seems to follow that true wisdom would direct us to that proceeding which tended most to conform with life, and to maintain in activity every portion of our frame and every branch of our nature. It is thus that we shall most effectually counterwork an enemy who is ever in wait for us.

Another argument in favor of a certain degree of attention to be paid to, and cultivation to be bestowed upon, sensible pleasures is, that the sensations of our animal frame make an important part of the materials of our knowledge. It is from sense that we must derive those images which so eminently elucidate every department of science. One of the great objects, both of natural science and morality, is to judge of our sensible impressions. The man who has not yielded a due attention to them would in vain attempt to form an enlightened judgment on the question we are here attempting to discuss. There is a vast variety of topics that he would be disqualified to treat of or to estimate.

Excessive drinking usually leads men into debauched company and unprofitable conversation. It inevitably impairs, in a greater or less degree, the intellectual faculties, and probably always shortens the life of the person addicted to it, a circumstance particularly to be regretted when that life is eminently a useful one. Gaming, besides the bad company to which it inures a man, — of persons who can scarcely be said to redeem their guilt in this respect by many virtues, — accustoms him to some of the worst habits of mind, induces him to seek and to rejoice in the misfortunes of others.

LIBERTY — REASON — JUSTICE — SOCIETY.

Every man has some idea of the advantages of liberty; but, for the most part, he has been instructed to believe that men would tear each other to pieces, if they had not priests to direct their consciences, and lords to consult for their subsistence, and kings to steer them in safety through the inexplicable dangers of the political ocean. But, whether they be misled by these or other prejudices, whatever be the fancied terror that induces them quietly to submit to have their hands bound behind them, and the scourge vibrated over their heads, all these are questions of reason. Truth may be presented to them in such irresistible evidence, perhaps by such just degrees familiarized to their apprehension, as ultimately to conquer the most obstinate prepossession.

The Armenians in the East are as universally distinguished among the nations with whom they reside, as the Jews in Europe; but the Armenians are as much noted for probity as the Jews for thrift. What resemblance is there between the ancient and the modern Greek, between the old Romans and the present inhabitants of Italy, between the Gauls and the French? Diodorus Siculus describes the Gauls as particularly given to taciturnity, and Aristotle affirms that they are the only warlike nation who are negligent of women.

Can there be any state of mankind that renders them incapable of the exercise of reason? Can there be a period in which it is necessary to hold the human species in a condition of pupilage? If there be, it seems but reasonable that their superintendents and guardians, as in the case of infants of another sort, should provide the means of their subsistence without calling upon them for the exertion of manual industry. Wherever men are competent to look the first duties of humanity in the face, and to provide for their defence against the invasions of hunger and the inclemencies of the sky, there they will, beyond all doubt, be found equally capable of every other exertion that may be necessary to their security and welfare. Present to them a constitution that shall put them into a simple and intelligible way of directing their own affairs, adjudging their contests among themselves, and cherishing in their bosoms a manly sense of dignity, equality, and independence, and you need not doubt that prosperity and virtue will be the result. We will suppose that it is right for one man to possess a greater portion of property than another, either as the fruit of his industry or the inheritance of his ancestors. Justice obliges him to regard this property as a trust, and calls upon him maturely to consider in what manner it may best be employed for the increase of liberty, virtue, and knowledge. He has no right to dispose of a shilling of it at the will of his caprice merely. So far from being entitled to well-earned applause for having employed some scanty pittance in the service of philanthropy, he is in the eyes of justice a delinquent if he withhold any portion from that service. In the same manner as his property, he should hold his person as a trust in behalf of mankind. He is bound to employ his talents, his understanding, his strength, and his time, for the production of the greatest quantity of general good. Such are the declarations of justice; so great is the extent of duty.

Society is nothing more than an aggregation of individuals. Its claims and its duties must be the aggregate of their claims and duties — the one no more precarious and arbitrary than the other. What has society a right to require from a man? The question is already answered: everything that it is his duty to do. Anything more? Certainly not. Can they change eternal truth, or subvert the nature of man? Can they make it his duty to be intemperate, to maltreat or assassinate his neighbor? Again: what is it that society is bound to do for its members? Everything that can contribute to their welfare. But the nature of their welfare is defined by the nature of mind. That will most contribute to it which enlarges the understanding, supplies incitements to virtue, fills us with a generous consciousness of our own independence, and carefully removes whatever can impede our exertions.

IMAGINATION.

This word — imagination — is derived from the Latin word *imago*, an image, which signifies the resemblance of some original thing. There can be no proper action of this faculty but as an adequate resemblance of some palpable object, as there can be no image or resemblance where there is no original; but its qualities may be varied by new combinations. Pythagoras, who discovered the property of the hypothenuse, did not create it; Faustus, who discovered or invented printing, did not create the properties of the press; and Lycurgus, who established the constitution of Sparta, created no new faculty in man or Nature.

The inhabitant of this world, in the development of his energy to augment good and diminish evil on earth, can receive no aid from the people of Saturn, or the number of the stars; and hence, it would be better for man, admonished by this lesson, to study himself on the ample experience of sensation as the all-sufficient science of self and Nature. All qualities or powers must have substance or extension to exist in; and thought or mind is the substance of the brain in action, though the understanding of man may be incapable of discovering by what subtle process matter modifies itself into thought.

The word "ghost" is a phantasm, involving a contradiction, and means a dead body performing the functions of life. The word "apparition" implies the contradiction that one and the same body can be or exist in two places at the same time, as when a sick man in New York appears to a friend in Boston, to predict the death of either of the parties; and though the prediction may happen to come true, the falsehood of the vision or phantasm would still be the same. The truth of the prediction is nothing more than an extraordinary concurrence of circumstances which exist in the chapter of accidents or chances.

Almost every man is in the habit of thinking of his absent friends, in their relative circumstances of health, riches, happiness, sickness, adversity, and death. In that part of the globe called Europe, about two hundred millions of people are living in intellectual intercourse, by means of the press, thinking of the fate of absent friends in every possible combination of circumstances. So long as their conjectures are false and disappointed, they are passed over silently;

but should one come true in the course of twenty years, the papers of the civilized world proclaim the occurrence as a miracle, when it would be more miraculous if such wonderful occurrence did not take place, considering the number of dreams and the length of time.

Let us look at this matter a little more closely. Every hundredth person, we will suppose, is engaged in thinking of the fate of an absent friend; here, then, we have two millions of people, three hundred and sixty-five times in the year, for the course of twenty years, thinking, dreaming, and seeing visions. One receives a letter from a sick friend, and thinks he is dead; another dreams he died on such a night; a third saw an apparition, that is, an idea came across his mind that his friend died at a certain instant of time, which proved to be true. This occurrence, however extraordinary, is not at all unaccountable or miraculous, because, taking into the estimate the number of two millions that think every day in the year upon the same subject, it would not be above ten or twenty chances to one, that a series of events should occur at the same instant in the course of twenty years, as that a person should think of the death of his friend at the very day or hour when he died, particularly if in ill health, or exposed to danger; or that a concurrence of events should take place, such as a vision or a freak of fancy, or a noise at the door by the cat, which awoke the dreamer about the time when his friend expired.

This plain and simple calculation of chances to account for predictions will convince, we should suppose, any intelligent and reflecting man, that any prediction of events which cannot connect the means with its end is nothing more than a conjecture at hazard, which the table of chances may verify without causing wonder or stupefaction in rational or well-disciplined understandings.

The word "witch" is another phantasm when used with the import of vulgar apprehensions, which means an ugly old woman in possession of supernatural power; that is, having power above her nature, or having what she cannot have, — a palpable contradiction. This observation will apply to the whole vocabulary of phantasms, such as magic, prophecy, inspiration, incantation, etc., etc., which are all words of contradictory import, signifying ends without means, or power beyond possibility.

The fancy is an arbitrary creator of notions, or thoughts without object, useful to amuse in poetry or instruct in fables. Its power is augmented by reading books of fiction, and its evil influence in disposing the mind to superstition and credulity might be guarded against by an avowal of its fictitious nature by those authors who use it to personify all modes of existence.

LITERATURE — EDUCATION — JUSTICE.

There are three principal causes by which the human mind is advanced towards a state of perfection; literature, or the diffusion of knowledge through the medium of discussion, written or oral; education, or a system for the early impression of right principles upon the hitherto unprejudiced mind; and political justice, or the adoption of any principle of morality and truth into the practice of a community.

Literature has reconciled the whole thinking world respecting the great principles of the system of the universe, and extirpated on this subject the dreams of romance and the dogmas of superstition. Literature has unfolded the nature of the human mind, and Locke and others have established certain maxims respecting man, as Newton has done respecting matter, that are generally admitted as unquestionable. Discussion has ascertained with tolerable perspicuity the preference of liberty over slavery. Local prejudice had introduced innumerable privileges and prohibitions upon the subject of trade; speculation is beginning to ascertain that freedom is more favorable to her prosperity.

Where must the preceptor himself have been educated, who shall elevate his pupil above all the errors of mankind? If the world be full of intrigue and rivalship and selfishness, he will not be wholly disinterested. If falsehood be with mankind at large reduced to a system, recommended by the prudent, commanded by the magistrate, enforced by moralists and practised under a thousand forms, the individual will not always have the simplicity to be sincere, or the courage to be true. If prejudice has usurped the seat of knowledge, if law and religion and metaphysics and government be surrounded with mystery and artifice, he will not know the truth, and therefore cannot teach it; he will not possess the criterion, and therefore cannot furnish it to others.

Superstition, an immoderate fear of shame, and a false calculation of interest are errors that have been always attended with the most extensive consequences. How incredible, at the present day, do the effects of superstition exhibited in the Middle Ages, the horrors of excommunication and interdict, and the humiliation of the greatest monarchs at the feet of the pope, appear! What can be more contrary to our customs and modes than that dread of disgrace which formerly induced the Brahmin widows of Hindostan to destroy themselves upon the funeral pile of their husbands? What more glaringly immoral than the mistaken idea which leads multitudes in commercial countries to regard fraud, falsehood, and circumvention as the truest policy? But, however powerful these errors may be, the empire of truth, if once established, would be far greater. A system of government that should lend no sanction to ideas of fanaticism and hypocrisy would soon accustom its subjects to think justly upon topics of moral worth and importance. A state that should abstain from imposing contradictory and impracticable oaths, and thus perpetually stimulating its members to concealment and perjury, would soon become distinguished by plain dealing and veracity. A country in which places of dignity and confidence should cease to be at the disposal of faction, favor, and interest, would not long be the residence of servility and deceit.

If every man could with perfect facility obtain the necessaries of life, and, obtaining them, feel no uneasy craving after its superfluities, temptation would lose its power. Private interest would visibly accord with public good, and civil society become all that poetry has feigned of the golden age.

WORDS — IDEAS.

Language, in all its dialects, has been gradually formed by the various wants and whims of human beings. That it required no supernatural inspiration must be evident from the more recondite discoveries and complicated inventions of human ingenuity. The function of speech, that is, its nature and end, is to communicate the operations of one mind to the intelligence of another. Certain words are established as the representative signs of things, and when uttered by the mouth or exhibited in writing or printing, we receive them as the exposition of things or their corresponding thoughts.

All Nature is comprehended in the term physics, which means the laws or course of matter and power, — that is, substance and its qualities as exhibited in their phenomena and verified by experience. The word metaphysics has been used and abused as a vain and futile distinction applied to qualities alone, as to heat in the body of the sun, or thought in the body of man. The quality of heat is as substantial a phenomenon, presented to the sense of feeling, as the body of the sun to the sense of sight; they are both physical essences, and stand in no need of the useless distinction of the word metaphysics. In the same manner, the quality of thought in the human brain is as much a physical action as the circulation of the blood, and exhibits its phenomena with the same palpable sense and intelligence, to be verified by the test of experience, and therefore the word metaphysics is a misapplied and useless distinction in real knowledge, and should be confined to those impenetrable secrets of Nature which are concealed from the human species, because they would avail nothing, if understood or known, towards producing the general harmony of existence; that is, the augmentation of good, and the diminution of evil in the present state of being.

The mythology of gods, goddesses, celestial senates, demons, etc., drawn from human imagination, is vague hypothesis, characterized by a set of words without meaning, and sounds without sense, which can have no import in human language, as they represent no phenomena, no objects, and no relations amenable to the test of experience. The words virtue and vice, or good and evil, are perpetually interchanging their limits, and varying their identities in the incessant mutability of circumstances. Falsehood, or lying, is a great vice; but the suppression of truth may sometimes be required by necessity.

Secrecy is often the basis of confidence, and a great virtue. War is no doubt an evil; but if the advancement of right, and diminution of wrong in the mundane system require war in the defence of social and political life, it becomes a good, as peace would become an evil, if adopted in such a case.

The first rule to make language represent realities instead of phantoms may be exemplified by considering the oratorical, rhetorical, and eloquent absurdities of metaphysicians, from the great prototype Plato, down to the modern Locke. What volumes of erudite contention in words, simply, have been produced and disciplined by logic, both scholastic and natural, so called by Locke, to prove that we have ideas in the mind without things, their prototypes! that is, copies without originals — downright contradictions, calculated to deprave human reason, and produce a state of universal confusion. The mind has no power to create original objects or ideas; and even their remote and projected relations, which appear as simple acts of thought, are all suggested by the objects themselves in their capacities, and therefore copied, and not created by the fiat of the mind; and the most complicated systems of moral institutions are nothing but the development of human energy, detected and discovered by genius in the suggested and projected relations of the capacity or the constitution of man.

The other essential rule of the art of reasoning is, to consider in full evidence all the parts or subjects of propositions. The moral science resembles the mathematical science; no part in a demonstration can be fully understood unless we embrace the whole; and as the elements and system of the first have never yet been fully understood by mankind, all its words and terms are but dialects of local education, customs, and knowledge; and whoever attempts to pass beyond these must speak to his countrymen an unknown language, and can be intelligible only to travellers who have no country, or philosophers who have no prejudice. When we take any proposition into contemplation, we should meet it in the calm temperament with which we view a mathematical problem. No man feels a bias or emotion upon such inquiry, and therefore the question is solved with irrefutable accuracy.

MAKE THE BEST OF EVERYTHING.

An important lesson to learn, and the earlier in life it is learned the better, is to *make the best of everything*. As the old adage says, "There is no use in crying over spilt milk." Misfortunes that have already happened, cannot be prevented, and, therefore, the wise man, instead of wasting his time in regrets, will set himself to work to recover his losses. The mistakes and follies of the past may teach us to be more cautious for the future; but they should never be allowed to paralyze our energies, or surrender us to weak repinings. A millionaire of this city (Boston) tells the story that at one period, early in his career, he had got almost to the verge of bankruptcy; "But," says he, "I ploughed a deep keel, and kept my own counsel," and by these means he soon recovered. Had this man given way to despair; had he sat down to bewail his apparently impending ruin, he might now have been old and poor, instead of a capitalist in a leading position. He adds that his characteristic was that through life, in all circumstances, he did the best that he could, whatever that was, consuming no time in useless regrets over bad speculations.

The rule holds good, not only in mercantile

affairs, but in the whole conduct of life. The man who is born to indifferent circumstances will never rise, if, abandoning himself to envy of those more blessed by fortune, he goes about sullenly complaining, instead of endeavoring to use to the best of his ability what few advantages he has. The patriot, deploring the decline of public and private morals, will never succeed in reforming the commonwealth if he stickles for visionary or impracticable measures, rejecting those more moderate ones which are really attainable. The friend will soon have no intimates at all if, making no allowance for the infirmities of human nature, he judges too harshly the conduct of his acquaintances. Many a matrimonial separation might be avoided, if husband and wife, instead of taking offence at each other at slight provocation, would dwell rather on the good traits their partner displays. There are not a few statesmen now living in retirement, who might have still gratified their ambition by serving the public, if they had understood, amid the intrigues and disappointments of public life, how to make the best of everything. We never see a man bewailing his ill fortune without something of contempt for his weakness. No individual or nation ever rose to eminence in any department, which gave itself up to this childish behavior. Greatness can only be achieved by being superior to misfortunes, and by returning again and again to the assault with renewed energy. And this it is which is truly *making the best of everything.*

INTELLECTUAL IMPROVEMENT.

The citizens of this republic enjoy a greater degree of freedom, apparently, than any other people on the globe; and yet, the fundamental basis of our Constitution, that "All men are created equal," is every day practically violated. As it respects what are termed the *common* people, we are *theoretically* free, but *practically* we are slaves, — slaves to unequal laws, — slaves consequently to the rich, by whose influence and for whose benefit, those laws are framed. We are slaves to their will and pleasure, and harnessed to their car of party. The only hope of deliverance rests on the march of knowledge, that gives light to the understanding, calls the moral energies of man into action, elevates him to his proper dignity, and will eventually nerve his arm with power to break the fetters from his limbs, that will enable him to stand forth in the full growth of human intellect — a FREEMAN.

We may depend upon it, if ever mankind shall enjoy the full extent of political freedom and equality, they must be acquired by individual exertion, to form such characters as will qualify us to contend for, and make us worthy to inherit the blessing, as the only means of wresting it from the clutches of aspiring demagogues. If the poor shall ever be emancipated from the oppression of the rich, and peace, plenty, and contentment bless the community,— if bickering and strife be ever banished, and pure social happiness prevail, the great and important work must be accomplished by the same great means, INTELLECTUAL IMPROVEMENT.

ACTIONS — DUTIES — VIRTUES.

The bad practice of duelling was originally invented by barbarians for the gratification of revenge. It was probably at that time thought a very happy project for reconciling the odiousness of malignity with the gallantry of courage. But in this light it is now generally given up. Men of the best understanding who at this day lend it their sanction are unwillingly induced to do so, and engage in single combat merely that their reputation may sustain no slander.

Which of these two actions is the truest test of courage; the engaging in a practice which our judgment disapproves, because we cannot submit to the consequences of following that judgment, or the doing what we believe to be right, and cheerfully encountering all the consequences that may be annexed to the practice of virtue? With what patience and satisfaction can a man of virtue think of cutting off the life of a fellow-mortal, or of putting an abrupt close to all the generous projects he may himself conceive for the benefit of others, merely because he has not firmness enough to awe impertinence and falsehood into silence?

The worst actions, the most contrary to abstract justice and utility have no doubt been done from conscientious motives. Ravillac, Clement, Damiens, had their minds deeply penetrated with anxiety for the eternal welfare of mankind; for this object they sacrificed their ease, and cheerfully exposed themselves to torture and death. It was benevolence, probably — as taught by the Christian religion of the time — that contributed to light the fires of Smithfield, and point the daggers of Saint Bartholomew. The inventors of the gunpowder plot in England were, in general, men remarkable for the sanctity of their lives and the severity of their manners. And so, likewise, the murderer of President Lincoln may have thought, from the influences by which he was surrounded, that he was right and acting conscientiously in becoming an assassin. Thus it is that an action, though done with the best intention in the world, may have nothing in it of the nature of virtue.

John Calvin, we will suppose, was clearly and conscientiously persuaded that he ought to burn Michael Servetus. Ought he to have burned him or not? If he burned him, he did an action detestable in its own nature; if he refrained, he acted in opposition to the best judgment of his own understanding as to a point of moral obligation. It is absurd, however, to say, that it was in any sense his duty to burn him. Therefore, we conclude that the most essential part of virtue consists in the incessantly seeking to inform ourselves more accurately upon the subject of utility and right. Whoever is greatly misinformed respecting this subject, is indebted for his error to a defect in his philanthropy and zeal.

Since absolute virtue may be out of the power of a human being, it becomes us in the meantime to lay the greatest stress upon a virtuous disposition, which is not attended with the same ambiguity. A virtuous disposition is of the utmost consequence, since it will in the majority of instances be productive of virtuous actions; since it tends, in exact proportion to the quantity of virtue, to increase our discernment and improve our understanding; and since, if it were but universally propagated, it would immediately lead to the great end of virtuous actions, the purest and most exquisite happiness of intelligent beings.

From these simple principles we may deduce the moral equality of mankind. We are partakers of a common nature, and the same causes that contribute to the benefit of one, contribute to the benefit of another. Our senses and faculties are of the same denomination. Our pleasures and pains will therefore be the same. We are all of us endowed with reason, able to compare, to judge, and to infer. The improvement, therefore, which is to be desired for the one is to be desired for the other. We shall be provident for ourselves, and useful to each other, in proportion as we rise above the atmosphere of prejudice. The same independence, the same freedom from any such restraint as should prevent us from giving the reins to our own understanding, or from uttering upon all occasions whatever we think to be true, will conduce to the improvement of all.

The thing really to be desired, is the removing, as much as possible, arbitrary distinctions, and leaving to talents and virtue the field of exertion unimpaired. We should endeavor to afford to all, the same opportunities and the same encouragement, and to render justice the common interest and choice. Persecution cannot persuade the understanding, even when it subdues our resolution. It may make us hypocrites, but cannot make us converts. The government, therefore, which is anxious above all things to imbue its subjects with integrity and virtue will be the farthest in the world from discouraging them in the explicit avowal of their sentiments. It is only by giving a free scope to these excursions, that science, philosophy, and morals have arrived at their present degree of perfection, or are capable of going on to that still greater perfection, in comparison with which all that has been already done, will perhaps appear inferior and childish.

MOTHERS AND CHILDREN.

If it be a fact — and we believe it is generally conceded — that extraordinary men always have extraordinary mothers, or women of uncommon or superior minds, then it follows that in order to improve mankind, we must improve womankind; or perhaps we should say, improve the latter, first. Mothers, much more than fathers, mould the disposition and character of their children; and consequently, as an intelligent lady lately observed at a public meeting, "when mothers are properly educated, children will be brought up properly." She was exactly right. It is a good, useful, secular education that women most need, and not religion, — an education that shall teach them a knowledge of all those laws of their being on which health, life, happiness, prosperity, contentment, usefulness, longevity, in short, everything that makes life worth having, necessarily depends.

What is a belief in the "Trinity," or "Unity," or the "Virgin Mary," or the "Thirty-nine Articles," and all the rest of the dogmas and creeds of the churches, both Protestant and Catholic, in comparison with the possession of a good, strong, vigorous, handsome, healthy constitution, and the knowledge how to take care of it? Why, to our mind, the former is to the latter as mere dross to pure gold; and yet, in the religious world, the "house we live in," or the body, is hardly worth minding, while the "mansions in the sky," which "no eye hath seen" and probably never will see, are the only things deserving human attention. "So runs the world away," and humanity is cheated, fooled, humbugged, and plundered, while living, and at death is pointed to the imaginary Utopia above the clouds, for the enjoyment of that happiness, which, if society was rightly managed, might be enjoyed here, and the possession of which would make our earth a paradise, and hell a fable. Will humanity ever enjoy this happiness? We hope so, for it is "a consummation devoutly to be wished," but it is almost like hoping against hope to expect it; for when a man arises in society, whose love for humanity supersedes his respect for churches and creeds, the majority, who are always religious, become alarmed, and making common cause as it were against the daring innovator, exclaim, "This man is an infidel; come, let's kill him!"

But, though this is a part of our subject, we have somewhat disgressed from the leading idea with which we started, which was, the improvement of mothers and children; two very important branches of humanity, without whom the world would come to a standstill.

Now if it be a fact, as careful observers say it is, that by the manners of the children, we may judge of the temper of the mother, then of course her proper education by improving herself improves her offspring; thus making intellect, character, and organization to a great degree, if not entirely or wholly, hereditary. Washington's mother was a superior woman; so was Jefferson's, Franklin's, Bonaparte's, and so were the mothers of all the distinguished men who have made their mark on their country and the world and after generations. And here we are reminded of the truthful saying, as we believe, of that great and good man, the late Robert Owen, who, while faithfully laboring for more than half a century, and at an expense in money of half a million of dollars, as a social reformer, to benefit the condition of the workingmen of England, adopted the following as his motto, rule, and principle of moral and social action and reform: "The characters of men are formed *for* them, and not *by* them." We have often heard religious people scout this idea as very foolish, yet to our mind it is one of the best, because truest maxims ever uttered; and we are altogether mistaken if we have not seen it proved correct in many instances. How else, we would be glad to know, are we to account for the wealth, prosperity, fame, leisure, enjoyment of one class of people, and the poverty, vice, crime, misery, toil, and wretchedness of another and a larger class? Do people really desire the former, and wish to avoid the latter things? Undoubtedly.

Then how comes it about that so many possess the latter, and so few the former? In both cases it is owing to the force of circumstances, and we shall be satisfied of this fact in proportion as we become acquainted with the individual history of people belonging to these two classes. It seems to us as clear as the simplest sum in arithmetic that, given the social circumstances of a community or neighborhood, it is easy to determine their moral and intellectual condition. But we need not speculate theoretically on this point, for Mr. Owen has demonstrated it by the practical logic of incontrovertible facts. For a period of nearly twenty years he was the governor or manager of a laboring population of three thousand, whose social circumstances were made easy, pleasant, and agreeable, all their wants being satisfied. The consequence was there was no poverty, no ignorance, no excessive toil, none of the misery and wretchedness of the outside world, experienced in his village (New Lanark); the inhabitants were prosperous, contented, happy, and moral, so moral, in fact, that when commissioners of Parliament visited that town, among others, to report the number of criminals, they reported that in Mr. Owen's town there were no criminals. He had surrounded his people with such favorable circumstances that they had no inducement to commit crime, and hence they led moral lives. Here is the secret, and what circumstances have done for New Lanark, they will do for other localities; since as the evils of society are all of human instead of heavenly origin, a human remedy will remove them, and nothing else can. So when the doctrine of "circumstances" is properly understood and appreciated, it will be seen to be the only true panacea for social evils, and that as it contemplates the improvement of women as well as men, it will also benefit children, and thus all three classes will be saved with a reasonable, a practical, and a true salvation. It is of no use to look to heaven to find a remedy for the ills of this life; because, being of the "earth, earthy," they can only be cured by earthly means.

AMUSEMENTS ON SUNDAY.

The fact that public exercises are not countenanced on Sunday, except those which are strictly of a religious nature, leads to a public evil of which we would complain, namely, that as a large portion of our young men do not feel any interest in religious exercises, and consider all the time thus spent as so much wearisome confinement, they are accustomed to neglect them one half the day and to devote that time to some hurtful practice, for which they are not condemned because the fact is hid from observation.

We are all, probably, well acquainted with the fact, that in Puritanical communities, although there may be less vice than in other places, there is not *so much less* as there appears to be. An over-strictness in regard to the pleasures of mankind, while it diminishes public vice, increases private vice, though perhaps not in exactly the same ratio. Hence in the New England States there is probably more concealed vice than in France, though probably the sum of public and private vices added together is greater in the latter country. There is no propensity in the human heart, that we are aware of, to indulge in vice AS SUCH. There is simply a desire for pleasure, and this love of pleasure will lead to vice or innocent indulgence, just according to the nature of the laws and customs of the community. Men will have pleasures and amusements of one kind or another, on Sundays as well as on week days; but these need not be vicious unless the bad customs of society render them such.

Now there are two opposite kinds of society in which vice will be resorted to as an amusement. First, it will be resorted to in those communities in which all amusements of every kind are condemned, except those which arise from toil and the practice of devotion, as they were in the New England States under our ancestors, and still are in some old villages. Secondly, it will be resorted to in those communities in which vice itself is not condemned, so long as certain necessary laws for the protection of person and property are not violated. Such a state of things exists in some of the new States in North and South America.

The only state of society (if it is possible for *any* so to be) which can be kept free from vice is that in which the greatest possible amount of innocent amusements is both allowed and encouraged. No particular day of the week must be made an exception to this remark, for we must apply our remarks to human nature as it is, and not as we think it ought to be; and you cannot find an individual, except an enthusiast, or one who labors under a chronic state of moral or religious excitement, who is willing to spend a whole day of the week, that is, a seventh part of his life, in doing penance. Hence, if you afford men no entertainment on that day, except of a kind in which they do not and cannot feel the least interest, while you condemn likewise all such amusements as they may invent for themselves, you may be just as sure that they will indulge themselves in secret hurtful practices, as you can be of any fact which you witness with your own eyes.

This remark is not applicable to those, who, on account of having formed a taste for reading or some other rational amusement, can divert themselves in some one or other of these ways. Perhaps a majority of the elder portion of the community are so much fatigued with the labors of the week, that they are glad to spend the whole of the Sabbath literally as a day of rest, and while they appear to be deeply engaged in religious devotions, are really relieving a mind and a body that are exhausted with the toils of the past week. Such people do not need amusement, since to them, rest itself is the most agreeable reaction.

THE TRAINING OF CHILDREN.

Play is the natural employment of children. Systematic training is very prejudicial, because they do not understand the meaning nor the use of it, and have no liberty in it for mental exercise. The child's mind can only think of the child's own affairs; it cannot think of yours. In yours it is enslaved; in its own it is free. Body and mind, therefore, are better developed in managing a toy-horse, than in striving to fulfil an unchildish task; and it is only when both are freely developed together, that health can be enjoyed. For the sake of the promised manhood of boys, and the promised womanhood of girls, therefore, let all who can afford to bring up their children in a natural and healthy manner be cautious how they accept the theories of the precocious philosopher, or hasten to make phenomena of their children in early life. Remember that hasty growths are weakening to plants and animals, and the strongest and the most enduring are always those who slowly develop themselves.

Even the superior strength of man to woman is owing to this latter efflorescence; and it is no recommendation to any boy or girl, that they anticipate their years, and enact the part of man or woman before their time. Why, then, should education be hastened? Why should it be forced upon the infant mind, and why should that helpless and inexperienced mind be deprived of its natural rights of healthy, juvenile liberty, and childish excitement and enthusiasm, merely to gratify a morbid and unnatural parental desire of exhibiting it in a private family circle, as a surprising phenomenon? We should rather be ashamed of such phenomena — rather sorry for their misfortune in being phenomena, and check the rapidity of a morbid excitement that must speedily emerge in physical weakness and nervous irritability.

PHYSICAL EDUCATION.

The truth that the body is the only medium by which the mind communicates with earth, if not actually denied, is strangely overlooked by teachers generally. What the harp, flute, and organ, broken or untuned, are to the musician — the body, with its wonderful and scrupulously delicate functions, disabled or disorganized, is to the mind and heart. "A sound body for a sound mind," — here is the secret of a full, symmetrical, and correct appropriation of a man's physical and moral energies. The framework of the massive steamboat, must, for strength, be in proportion to the power of the engine, or the working of the latter will speedily break down the former. An active mind in a feeble body does the same.

Now if these are truthful and common-sense principles, then it follows that the building up and waxing mighty of the physical constitutions of the coming millions of our nation is an important, and in fact, an indispensable work; and it is a fortunate omen, that the facilities for intellectual and moral training are multiplying almost beyond degree. But without physical education, the human constitution will soon be overworked, since the facilities for propelling mind will prove as fuel to the steam-engine; they will increase action only to cause a speedier and more appalling ruin to the framework which sustains it. He, therefore, who does anything by publishing and revealing to families, especially to wives and mothers, judicious and healthful knowledge on physical education, is helping on the true salvation of our country and the world.

The great work must be, to enlighten parents. It is the rescue of the coming generations. It is the inculcation of the wholesome precepts of wisdom and prudence in regard to the prevailing errors respecting diet, dress, exercise, ventilation, reading, study, and morals. Society groans under a load of suffering inflicted by causes which might easily be removed, but which, in consequence of ignorance, fashion, prejudice, etc., are still permitted to operate. Therefore, we infidels, who believe in having good bodies as well as minds, can help to secure both, by promoting the great work of *Physical Education.*

REFORM.

The world can be refined and improved only by the removal of absurd notions, principles, and customs, and the adoption of good ones. Hence may be perceived the utility and importance of the enthusiastic exertions of isolated individuals of inventive and discriminative powers in the wide fields of reform; for, by the perseverance and determination of a few philosophic philanthropists, the moral world may, before many years, become sufficiently renovated and improved to render the virtuous successful, the honest happy, and the wise powerful.

THOUGHTS FOR THE YOUNG.

It is a common custom with editors of papers — secular as well as religious ones — to give advice to the rising generation, for in this particular, the press claims to be an instructor not less than the pulpit. And as we too have youthful readers, perhaps they will give attention to the following thoughts of an old friend of theirs, whose reflections and experience seem in his estimation to enable him to impart good advice, and who also sincerely wishes that their lives may be useful, prosperous, and happy.

How vastly important are the moments of youth! They constitute the best, if not the only time for the acquirement of everything that can elevate, adorn, and ennoble the human character. Yes, this is the fit period of your existence, not only for attaining valuable knowledge, and securing to yourselves virtue, wisdom, and lasting felicity, but now, also, is the season in which you must be wary and ever upon your guard lest you acquire and become fixed in the foolish habits and vicious customs of the society which surround you. For, whether you know it or not, it is a sad truth, that for one wise and virtuous individual that is to be found in the current pursuits of life, you will meet with, at least, seven who are either foolish or vicious. Therefore, avoid as far as possible, all intimacy and conversation with such individuals, that thereby you may remain secure from the contamination of their follies and vices, for let it be remembered, that you were born free from vice, and can be trained to virtue. Hence, it should be your assiduous duty to avoid the former and acquire the latter.

Then, in order to escape the evil and attain the good, strive to gain a taste and preserve a zest for thought and reflection, while youth, health, vigor and vivacity flow through your frames; for when youth is passed, the animal spirits begin to droop. Fail not then to appreciate your present, which, if once lost, becomes irrecoverable. Then deceive not yourselves, but remember that if you defer the acquisition of valuable knowledge, wise and virtuous habits, until mature age, you will labor under the double disadvantage of learning slowly and forgetting nearly as fast as you learn. Remember that early habits of industry and reflection, united with honesty, truthfulness, temperance, kindness, justice, and all the other useful, practical, human virtues which benefit ourselves and our fellow-men, will enable you to be and to feel much more independent, exalted, and happy, than can the mere possession of wealth and the ability of moving in the giddy circles of pomp and fashion.

Beyond the necessaries of life, it is not important that the pecuniary means of the habitually industrious, reflective, and wise, should be large. Money, however, when honestly earned, is a good thing, because it can be made useful to ourselves and to others; to ourselves when we are past labor, and to others, when it enables us to lend a helping hand to the poor and unfortunate. Be active, then, in your business, and when you have acquired a competence, be prudent in the saving and judicious in the disbursement of it. Do not be anxious at any time on the score of instruction or the right kind of teaching, for you will always have a full and perfect library around you which comprises the most valuable of all books — we mean the great volume of Nature. Never doubt the truth of this statement, nor lose sight of its great and paramount importance, but ever be assured that the pure study of Nature, of all other studies, is the most important, for it will never inspire you with fanaticism and an evil spirit, nor will it ever mislead you; but, on the contrary, the contemplation of Nature must always tend to humanize, refine, and exalt your character.

If you enjoy good health, and possess an ordinary share of intellectual capability, and begin in early life to be studious, thoughtful, and reflective, by thirty years of age, each of you may become like a host in valuable knowledge, mental power, and moral influence; and consequently will establish yourselves in principles that have the immutable rock of truth for their basis.

It is all important, you see, that you *begin right*, for human life is a succession of parts — infancy, youth, manhood, maturity, decline, old age, and death. What a man becomes, depends on education, and other circumstances that surround him; as his infancy is, so will be his youth; as his youth is, so will be his manhood; as his manhood is, so will be his maturity; as maturity is, so will be decline; as decline is, so will be old age. Then if youth be passed in idleness, ignorance, folly, and vice, how can one hold his way in the world, side by side with the intelligent, the worthy, and the virtuous? If manhood has been passed in low pursuits, in establishing in the heart, evil propensities, in wasting natural vigor, what awaits one in old age, but poverty, pity, and contempt? But if youth be devoted to the reasonable cultivation of the physical and intellectual powers, if knowledge of human duty be acquired and rightly used, manhood will be worthy; maturity, respectable; decline, honored; and old age, venerable.

THE RIGHT TO EXPRESS OPINIONS.

One of the most important rights which human beings possess, abstractly, and which ought to be guaranteed to them by the society of which they are members, is, the right to express opinions, without fear or molestation. That men ought to possess this right, not only as a matter of abstract justice, but as a matter of political expediency, is a proposition which carries its own evidence along with it. The right to think freely upon all subjects belongs to us naturally, and no government can deprive us of it. Now the right to think involves the right to express our opinions; for if we were to be deprived of the power of communicating our ideas to each other, we should be unable to benefit society by developing truths which we might discover.

The right to express opinions on all subjects,

save religion and politics, is conceded by almost all governments to their people. The autocracy of Russia, and the paternal despotism of Austria, prohibit discussion among the people on political affairs, and England and our own country sometimes punish those who dare to express opinions derogatory to Christianity. The persecution of Abner Kneeland for blasphemy, — the statute against which unmeaning crime is not even yet repealed, — proves the correctness of the latter statement. A brief examination of the principal arguments usually urged in defence of such prosecutions, may suffice to show their injustice, and to place the right of man to the unrestricted expression of opinion in a clear light: —

First. — It is said that if men were permitted to publish opinions derogatory to religion, the public would be induced to regard it with contempt. To this it may be replied, that religion must be a thing in itself contemptible, or the public intellect must be very defectively educated, or such an effect would never be produced. Every prosecution for the undefinable crime of blasphemy, therefore, is a tacit acknowledgment that the government and the priesthood have not done their duty in educating the people; or it is a tacit acknowledgment that religion is not founded in argument, and that it requires the terrors of corporal punishment for its support. Hence all such prosecutions are the most bitter and galling satires which could be launched against the government, priests, and religion.

Second. — It has been urged that the moral sense of the community is outraged by the publication of libels on religion, and that it is fitting and right that the publishers of such libels should be prosecuted. We see no force in this argument, because almost everything that a man might say of religion, while exercising his right of free inquiry, could be construed by the law and the church into a libel. Now it is well known that free inquiry has been instrumental in establishing science, in reforming jurisprudence, and in effecting the partial abloition of superstitious absurdities. It cannot therefore, do any harm to religion, if religion is founded in truth; and if not, free inquiry will expose its errors, and consequently ought to be encouraged. Moreover, the nature of belief is involuntary and proportionate to the amount and clearness of the evidence presented to the mind; hence it is unjust to punish a man for entertaining any opinion. Besides, as the individual right to inquire after truth obviously implies the right to express without fear the results of inquiry; so it may be argued that those who could restrict the free expression of opinion must either deny the abstract right of man to inquire after truth, or act inconsistently by denying in practice the right which the former involves. And finally, as truth is always beneficial, and error always pernicious to society, and as inquiry is the only mode by which we can ever arrive at truth, so all attempts to restrict inquiry are wrong and unjust.

These are some of the grounds upon which the right to free inquiry and to the free expression of opinion may be defended. And in view of them we may ask, why allow statutes to remain unrepealed, which are obnoxious to reason, and contrary to common sense? Does Christianity require the strong arm of the law to prop it up? We should think not, if it is from Heaven. Why, then, do professed Christians persecute unbelievers? For no other purpose, it would seem, than to gratify a thirst for vengeance, which their principles and religion are unable to repress.

PREACHING.

Perhaps for some years to come the practice of preaching will continue; but if it improves for the next quarter of a century as much as it has during the last quarter, it will probably be then a comparatively useful mode of public teaching. Its present improvement is owing not to the intrinsic merit of the Bible or religion, but to the outside pressure of Liberalism or Infidelity, which has compelled the pulpit, in order to preserve itself, to take an advanced position more in accordance with the growing liberality, intelligence, and toleration of the times. This regenerating influence must continue, and it must increase, for "revolutions [particularly of this kind] never go backwards"; and hence the prospect is, that if, in coming generations, there is to be any pulpit at all, it must be founded on the facts of reason instead of the fancies of a superstitious faith.

The pulpit-reform has already commenced, and "things are working" favorably. People are becoming more intelligent, inquisitive, and reflecting; consequently, preaching is rather a different affair from what it once was. Nowadays, people expect to be instructed, convinced, and persuaded by knowledge, reason, and argument. They are not satisfied with mere verbiage; they are not moved by empty or unmeaning declamation; they are not alarmed by sepulchral tones and unearthly grimaces. The demands of the community in regard to the character of public services are continually rising with the improvements of the community in every branch of science, and in the arts and distinctions of civilized life. You may now go into a church where once you would expect to hear denunciatory and controversial preaching, and not much will be uttered to offend a liberal mind, except now and then a keynote may be touched or an ear-mark shown, lest the minister's soundness should come under suspicion, or he should lose sight of his own identity. This is considerable gain — a gain to liberality and happiness.

What will do the people good? What will be the most useful? What will make them wiser, better, and happier? We know of no other rule than this by which the propriety and value of preaching is to be tested. And it is an encouraging sign of the times that preaching is becoming more and more in accordance with this rule. The polemical and denunciatory style of preaching, which served only to nourish spiritual pride and to kindle the vindictive passions, has in a great measure ceased. Here and there occasionally you may hear the straggling fires of some scattered portions of a retreating enemy; brave men who are not willing to quit the field until their last rounds are expended, though they fire them into the air. Here and there some veteran of the last wars, some Greenwich pensioner, who, fired with the indomitable spirit of his youth, " loves to shoulder his crutch and show how fields were won," may figure out to the amusement of the religious, and to the grief of the serious, who have ceased to be alarmed by the manœuvres of the most skilful tactician. But this denunciatory and controversial preaching has almost ceased. The growing intelligence of the people, and that which is its usual concomitant, the spirit of free inquiry and independent judgment, have put it down, and many of its warmest friends have been as anxious, as their consistency would allow them to be, to have it put down, because they found it was putting them down.

What are most requisite in a public teacher, are clearness of perception and soundness of judgment; a love of truth which nothing can quench; a sagacity in discerning, and a fearlessness in avowing it, which becomes those who understand its proper value; and these, when joined to industry and perseverance, afford the fairest promise of usefulness.

THE SUPPLY OF NATURAL WANTS.

Man requires the full supply of his physical necessities, and as he has hitherto remained in an antagonistic position to his fellow-beings, he finds it necessary to secure for his own use as much property as he can procure. If the full supply of his wants were to be guaranteed to him by society he would not be likely to amass wealth which he could not consume.

There are, however, several influences which may induce a man to grasp after wealth, independent of the desire to supply his natural wants. Wealth gives a man power over the labor of his fellow-beings, affords him respectability in society, and enables him to gratify his pride by living in the fashion. The consideration of these advantages exercises a powerful influence over many minds. There are thousands, if not tens of thousands, who prefer the indulgence of their pride, their ambition, and their selfishness to the promotion of the public welfare. Whether this results from the peculiarity of their cranial development, or from an evil training, or from the influence of local circumstances, there can be no doubt of the reality of the fact. The conduct of men, in this respect serves to show the nature of the influences by which they are actuated, and the existence of those influences explains the reason why men endeavor to acquire private posessions.

But, independent of the simple desire to secure the supply of our natural wants, of course including the wants of those with whom we are most intimate, all the other motives we have alluded to are impure and ignoble. What, are ambition, avarice, the love of power, the desire of show, in accordance, exclusively, with man's moral being? Forbid it, justice, philanthropy and truth! It would indeed be a lamentable chapter in the history of the human race if these characteristics of an ill-trained humanity were so essentially inwoven in the texture of our moral nature as not to admit of eradication. That men have been ambitious is admissible; that they are so essentially, and without a possibility of cure, is an unprovable assumption. That insatiable avarice, like a fell monster, has breathed upon the hearts of some men, and turned their natural warmth into frost, and their sweetness into gall, is an assertion warranted by the conduct of many individuals. This, however, affords no proof of the assumption that avarice belongs essentially to human nature. All these bad and injurious passions and propensities result from the training we receive, and the evil influences that operate upon us throughout life.

That ambition, avarice, and other evil passions, are mere accidents which the progress of the mind in knowledge and philosophy gradually removes, is a fact fully attested by the annals of private life. Are there not hundreds of individuals who would expend their resources in the relief of distress? Is there no sympathy, no affection, no philanthropy in the world? Does the human heart never feel the soft impulses of generosity? Has benevolence been confined to the breasts of Howard, Clarkson, Wilberforce, Owen and Girard? Is human nature a soil adapted to afford nutrition to every noxious plant, and not fitted to afford nourishment to those virtues that adorn the character and make us feel proud of our humanity? No! These suppositions are degrading to our nature, contradictory to facts, and inimical to virtue.

If, however, it be admitted that human nature is essentially good, and that there is in man a natural principle of benevolence, it will follow that the system of private property, instead of being in accordance with the nature of man, is directly opposed to it. The competitive system causes many to be in want of the necessaries of life, and the natural benevolence of the human heart disposes us to commiserate and relieve the distresses of our fellow-men. But in hundreds of cases where this benevolent desire is felt, the means are wanting whereby it might be gratified. Private interests and domestic rights frequently interfere with our feelings of public philanthropy, so that when we would alleviate the sufferings of our fellow-men, we find it, in some cases, impolitic, and in others, impossible. Here it is obvious that the present system of society comes into direct collision with the noblest feelings of our nature.

Again: The poor are obliged to compete with each other; not with respect to the outlay of their moneyed capital, of which they are *minus*, but with respect to their labor, the only capital they have at their disposal.

It is obvious that in such a wearisome and protracted struggle for the goods of life, some must rise and others fall; some be enabled to gratify their inordinate avarice, and others be kept in poverty. Hence the system of competition is not in accordance with human nature, for, if that system enables some to rise in the scale of affluence, it depresses others in proportion. And if it be argued that the system is right because some rise, it may be argued that it is wrong because others fall.

The preceding observations imply that the system of private property cannot be defended on the ground of abstract correspondence with the moral nature of man. If, therefore, it be defensible at all, it must be on the score of its utility. If it be better fitted to promote the welfare of mankind than the co-operative system, then let it be preserved; but if not, it should be abolished, and a new order of things established in its place.

THE RIGHT TO GOOD GOVERNMENT.

One of the most important rights which belong to man as a member of society is *the right to good government.* It is quite evident, we think, that constituted as society is now, some kind of government is absolutely necessary to its well-being; and it is not less true, that whatever form of government any community may think proper to adopt, should be of the best character. A good government should possess, it seems to us, the following characteristics: —

First. — It should be cheap; for if the people should be immoderately taxed to support the government, the evils resulting from such a system would counterbalance the good.

Second. — It should be effective; for if such were not to be the case, it would be unable to benefit the people by enacting wise and well-arranged laws, and by enforcing their observance.

Third. — It should be disinterested as it regards

particular class interests, making laws not for the benefit of one particular portion of the community, but for the benefit of all.

Fourth. — It should be entirely elective; as the people would then occasionally have the power of ejecting from office those men who might betray a regardlessness of the public welfare.

Fifth. — It should truly represent all classes of the community; that is, the members should be elected to office by all who are capable of understanding political affairs. From this, it follows, that the right of voting should be given to all who are capable of exercising the suffrage.

It is unnecessary to examine the question as to the best form of government out of the many that have been adopted by mankind; for we are all agreed, we presume, that ours, or a republic, is the best; but still it has defects which will have to be remedied before it becomes the best, in its practical workings, which can be devised. The preceding characteristics of a good government will enable the reader to test the merits of all the forms of government which have been adopted by different nations. In addition to these, the following abstract rules are worthy of attention: —

First. — The great end for which government is instituted, is the promotion of the general welfare. If, therefore, any form of government fails to produce this effect, we may confidently pronounce that form of government to be defective.

Second. — The duty of a government is to secure to individuals the full enjoyment of their rights. If, therefore, any form of government should fail in this respect, it must be defective also.

Third. — It is the duty of a government to see that the people receive a good physical, mental, and moral training; and any government that neglects this important duty, must be defective.

Fourth. — It is the duty of a government to take all practicable steps which may tend to increase the production of wealth, and also to see that the wealth produced be properly distributed; in other words, that the wants of all be fully supplied. If any form of government tend to prevent this, or if any legislative assembly should feel unwilling to do it, that form of government must be defective, and the members of that legislative assembly ought to be deposed. This test is especially applicable to all governments which have (or might have if they only would) abundant facilities for the production of wealth at their disposal.

The preceding observations appear to us to embrace all the characteristics and all the duties of a good government. If, therefore, these characteristics can be found in any government, that government deserves to be supported, not by the bayonets of a hired soldiery, but by the affections of the people.

In conclusion, no nation can be truly happy or

prosperous while it remains destitute of any, or of all of the above-mentioned rights. They are absolutely necessary to the well-being of any people; they are what the human mind longs for; and what the onward march of genuine democracy and liberal principles will ultimately compel all governments to grant. No population can be truly happy under a government which provides merely for their animal enjoyments, but which, at the same time, represses the noble love of liberty by a systematic and slavish system of education. It is in this respect that the paternal despotism of Austria is defective. It provides for the people a supply of food and enjoyment, which is in itself an excellent thing. But it at the same time degrades the mentality of the people, by prohibiting as far as its power will permit, inquiry and discussion. We shall probably never have exactly the right kind of government until the promotion of the general good becomes the sole actuating principle of human conduct.

FEMALE INFLUENCE.

Woman has a far greater influence on the public morals than the ministers of religion, though whatever the latter may accomplish in this respect is commendable on their part, and we would not withhold from them the credit to which they are fairly entitled. Morality, and not religion, being "the one thing needful," those who promote the former, are the true benefactors of society. Now women have a greater influence for better or worse, than ministers, because, as one reason, the number of the first is very much larger than the second. Mothers, and next to them school-teachers, plant the seeds of nearly all the good and evil that exist in the world; and as there are probably a thousand mothers and teachers to one minister, they have an almost unlimited influence for good or evil, over the minds and hearts of those committed to their charge. May it not, therefore, be justly said that they plant the *seeds* of *nearly* all the good and evil in the world?

But female influence in the formation of the right kind of character, is as yet but little understood. The philosopher talks about it; the friends of education, the patriot, the philanthropist, and the minister proclaim it; almost everybody admits it; some even believe it;—and yet, what is done? Not much, comparatively; in fact, scarcely anything. Woman is not only unknown to the other sex, but to herself. She has no sort of conception of her powers, or responsibilities.

She does not dream of a tithe of the good she might accomplish. If you tell her that her influence is not less in the restoration, than in the fall of our race, she either misunderstands you or regards you as visionary. By her own mismanagement, and especially by the mismanagement of her constituted lord, she is still the creature, and, to a great extent the dupe, of fashion, frivolity, superstition, and priestcraft. We speak of the sex generally, knowing there are noble exceptions, and that they are every day becoming more numerous.

When the rights, duties, and capabilities of women are better understood by both sexes, there will be an improved state of things; society will be far in advance of what it is to-day; and female influence, enlightened and regenerated, will prove itself the true savior of mankind. It is all important, in the improvement and salvation of the race, that the mothers should be properly educated; for the maxim is not less correct now than when first proclaimed by Confucius, that " By the manners of the children we may judge of the temper of the mother."

IMPORTANCE OF COMMON SCHOOLS.

A great many people seem to think that the permanency of our free institutions, the durability of republicanism, and, in short, all the highest and best interests of the country, depend on *churches.* We are of the opinion that all of these important things depend on COMMON SCHOOLS. They are the people's colleges; the sun of the people's mind; the lamp of freedom. Perhaps nineteen out of every twenty persons in these United States are educated in common schools alone; not one out of twenty ever enters either academy or college. This fact in itself tells us, at once, that as is the common school so is the education of the American people. Yes, the education of this nation is that and that only, which the common schools are prepared to give. How many, who read these lines, ever received more? You may have educated yourselves after you left those schools, but did not even this depend on the education which you there received?

Look at the connection of common schools with social order and prosperity. The educated man and the educated woman have other sources of enjoyment and other subjects of conversation than their neighbor's characters; but leave the mind empty, and frivolous gossipping and tea-table chat will be the amusement of their leisure hours. There is nothing we hold important or useful in society, but it is connected more or less directly with our schools. We may pile all the hilltops with magnificent architecture, but let the plain, brick schoolhouse go down, and very soon all the columns and architraves and domes will tumble with it into ruin. What is the true foundation of a republic? It is the common school. If we would have the one stand firm, we must build the other deep and sure. To neglect common schools is as bad as to destroy; nay, it is even worse; for mal-information is worse than no information, just as hunger is preferable to poisoned food.

THE CLERGY AND REFORM.

The clergy are always enlisted on the conservative side of all questions. We do not mean to cast any severe reflections on the clergy, when we say, that from the very nature and circumstances of their office in this country, they are, and always must be, behind the age, while these circumstances continue, in all matters appertaining to genuine intellectual improvement, and in the species of moral improvement which arises out of philosophical inquiry. At the same time they will always, as a body, be in advance of the age in that kind of superficial morality which consists in the observance of the decencies of life, and of mere theological precepts. They were for a season behind the age in the temperance reform, because temperance is not a theological virtue, but a moral one. When the current of public opinion set that way, the clergy not only floated along with it, but they spread their sails and went ahead of it, in some instances.

Whenever any reform or innovation is attempted, which is opposed to the established prejudices of the community, the clergy will necessarily fall in with it only as fast as it gains the approbation of the people. All this arises very obviously from our republican system of supporting religion. Any individual of the clergy who should, by the new doctrines he preached, manifest himself in advance of his parishioners, would be immediately displaced for another whose opinions are as backward as the ruling members of the parish. And it is seldom a clergyman's personal popularity is great enough to preserve him in his situation, in spite of religious prejudice against him. This circumstance necessarily operates to drive all such as are in advance of the community out of the profession, unless they can submit to the practice of a certain degree of dissimulation. Miss Martineau was therefore uncharitable in mentioning this fact as a matter of reproach against the clergy. Every man in the community knows that the clergyman of a parish is settled over it by the people, with reference to his agreement with them in doctrine, and with the understanding that all his eloquence is to be used in assisting them to maintain their present views. Should he make any innovation in point of doctrine, he must wait until the majority are previously prepared for it, under the penalty of being turned out of his pulpit, or he must have the art of insinuating his new doctrines into their minds under the cover of some old worn-out superstition which shall serve to render it palatable. It is needless to remark, that, on this account, the change must necessarily occur in the minds of the people first, and that afterwards they will allow their pastor to change his views in conformity with theirs. How can we, under such circumstances, reproach the clergy with being behind the age? As well might we reproach the effect for not preceding the cause. Neither do we mean to accuse the clergy of insincerity; for this republican system of supporting religion (which is, after all, the best one) prevents those individuals who are in advance of the age from adopting the profession of divinity, and draws them into the ranks of one of the other professions.

VIRTUE AND VICE.

Morality, simply considered as the bond of society, has no more to do with a future life, than it had with a past one: men seldom act in the common concerns of the world, from the hope of a distant and uncertain reward:—they feel impelled by something more immediate and forcible. The laws which must ever govern human nature, exist in that nature itself. Man being what he is, his nature determines his morality, inasmuch as it determines the effect which every external or internal influence shall produce for good or for evil; if for good, that influence is virtuous; if for evil, it is vicious. Having discovered what impressions afford him true and permanent enjoyment, and what influences occasion him painful sensations, we deduce thence his rules of conduct. This appears to be the only reasonable method, for all the philosophy and all the religion in the world, will never be able to carry us beyond the usual course of experience, or give us measures of conduct and behavior different from those which are furnished by reflections on common life. No new fact can be inferred from the religious hypothesis; no event foreseen or foretold; no reward or punishment expected or dreaded beyond what is already known by practice and observation.

Moral conduct springs from the mutual wants and interests of mankind. It is each man's interest that his neighbor should be virtuous; hence each man knows that public opinion will approve his conduct, if virtuous, — reprobate it, if vicious. And whenever mankind at large perceive, and whenever legislators act upon the perception, that *virtue and vice exist solely with reference to the nature of human beings* — then may we expect to see truth and reason prevail in the world. Those rules of conduct only can rightly be called laws, which regulate human actions alike on one day as on another day; and in a nation calling itself a republic, the laws of Moses should have no validity in courts of law to authorize persecutions for the breach of superstitious customs. Our highest object and the end of our endeavors, should be to free our country from the exercise of all religious tests in all judicial proceedings, and from Sunday penalties which violate the simple and imprescriptible rights of man. The tyranny of priests is as odious and insufferable as that of kings. The attempt to justify the violation of natural liberty because the majority adhere to those Mosaical prescriptions which occasion it, only enhances the injustice.

When the priests and their supporters say, that "The dogma of future rewards and punishments is the bond of society, and that to overthrow this dogma of the evangelical economy would release three quarters of the Christian world from all restraint," they might with truth rather say, that their imposition would be overthrown, and that the tyrannical institutions and exercise of priestly power would be immediately set aside. Men for their own safety are interested in the observance of the obligations of civil order, and indeed, its infringement leads to strengthened measures for enforcing its provisions, and to their increased effect by the experience of their indispensability. He must be as great a simpleton who believes that there could possibly be a necessity for a general flood over the earth to execute vengeance on the offenders against natural morals, as he who gives credit to its physical possibility.

Experience teaches us that the calamities of mankind have sprung from their superstitious opinions. The ignorance of natural causes created gods, and imposture made them terrible. Mankind lived unhappy because they were taught from their infancy to think that God had condemned them to misery. They never entertained a wish to break their chains, because they were taught that devotion, the renouncing of reason, mental debility, and spiritual debasement were the only means of obtaining salvation.

PROVIDENCE.

It is plain that Providence never interferes to protect innocence, or to prevent mischief, either amongst the inferior animals or mankind. The more we examine into the animal world, the more we shall be convinced that every different species and individual is regulated by its own particular interest, without reference to the advantage of any other species or individual, and not by any interference of Providence. We may also observe that there are various species of animals which are formed by Nature, solely for the purpose of destroying others. Their claws, their mouths, their teeth, are exactly calculated for devouring; and their stomachs are so constituted that animal food is their only nourishment, and they would linger and die without it. Now if God, or Providence, had intended anything like peace and harmony to exist in the world, he would have so constituted animals of all kinds that they should feed on roots, vegetables, fruits, fungi, and other inanimate substances which should have been made to grow from the earth in sufficient abundance and variety for every description of animals. And the system of procreation might also have been so regulated that there never should have been too many nor too few animals in the world at one time; and then no one animal, nor species, nor genus of animals would have been the natural enemy of another; but the face of the earth would then have exhibited a busy scene of various animals, all living in perfect happiness.

The belief in a Providence is not consistent with the general laws of Nature, and those who profess to believe it act as if they believed it not. Such an absurd doctrine can only be useful to kings and priests, and other deceivers of mankind, who use the word Providence to give their transactions an authority that must not be called in question, and under which authority they carry on the most malevolent practices. Thus they screen themselves from public censure, as no person that believes in a regulating Providence will attach any blame to them. But it should be our business to banish from our midst all belief in a Providence, and to behave with prudence and sobriety in all our actions, to use our best endeavors in well-doing, and not allow ourselves to be duped by those who pretend that Providence regulates all the transactions of men in authority, however injurious to individuals or mankind in general. Let us, therefore, persevere with manly endeavor to be useful to ourselves and to our fellow-men, trusting nothing to any imaginary being called Providence.

EDITING.

The mind is so constituted as to require, like the body, alternate labor and repose. Those occupations which demand great and frequent efforts of the mind, if they allow it suitable seasons for relaxation, are not injurious to health. Judicious exercise is necessary for the healthful development and vigorous action of the mental as well as the physical constitution. The occupations of the lawyer, the divine, the farmer, and the mechanic, all afford the mind abundant periods of rest. But such is not the case with that of the editor. His overtasked intellect finds no repose. His duties must be performed continually, — most methodically. Whether he feels like mental exercise or not, whether sick or well, his articles must be written, and all his multifarious duties performed. These labors are certainly sufficient to break down an ordinary constitution, but when we add to them pecuniary disappointment and embarrassment, lack of expected appreciation, the indifference of friends and the sarcasm of enemies, we have satisfactory explanation of the causes which disappoint the hopes, and cut short the career of so great a portion of newspaper editors.

There is occasionally an editor endowed with a strong body and a well-poised mind, alike indifferent to censure and praise, satisfied with his own powers, neither allured by hope, nor alarmed by fears, who will triumph over all obstacles, and pursuing calmly the even tenor of his way, attain renown, wealth, and long life; but whilst such an individual may, like any other prodigy, occasionally be found, numbers will fall around him the victims of unrequited mental labor and disappointed hopes.

A CHEERFUL PHILOSOPHY.

Surely no doubt should be entertained that this life should be made a happy and a cheerful one, that all the faculties with which we are gifted should be cultivated and improved, and that all the means of rational and innocent pleasure should be cherished. Is the earth wrapped up in a gloomy mantle, or in a delightful verdure? Does the vegetable world put forth its leaves, its blossom and its fruits, and its delightful fragrance in sadness and mourning, or in joy and thanksgiving? Does the returning sleep of exhausted nature awaken emotions of distrust and despondency, or teach us a tranquillizing lesson of the change which is to happen in human existence? Does the storm of winter, and the snowy covering in which it clothes the earth, terrify us with the power of Nature, or awaken new thoughts of contentment and satisfaction? Is the animal world destined to pain and misery, or to pleasure and gladness? Which of its many tribes does not cling to life as a precious gift? Why, then, should man regard his God — if there be one — as a stern and inexorable tyrant, and not as a kind and beneficent sovereign over all the human race?

It is evident, we think, that this gloomy and absurd doctrine was originated and has been maintained by religion, and that it will continue until the religion which produced it is superseded by a liberal and rational philosophy. There is no reasonable doubt that this philosophy, when properly taught and understood, will diffuse itself, eventually, throughout the earth. However slowly that day may seem, to bigots and sectarians, to be coming, that day will finally come, and long before eighteen hundred years, or the time that Christianity has been upon the earth. Why has Liberalism made so little progress, comparatively, during eightteen centuries? This question can be satisfactorily answered only by recurrence to the history of the world during that long lapse of time in which Christianity was in the ascendant, and exercised supreme sway and dominion. If we had space for such a purpose now, it could be easily proved that it is rather wonderful that Liberalism has made so much, rather than that it has not made greater, progress. When it shall come to be fully understood as a matter in accordance with the highest development of human reason, there will be no cause of discouragement as to its universal diffusion.

It is an unquestionable truth that the best method of disseminating truth and virtue, is to cultivate the human mind and to impart to it comprehensive and philosophic knowledge. The wisest men are the best men, but as there are many different constructions of the nature and obligations of the Christian faith, they cannot all be best, and we doubt whether any one of them is. That system of teaching and morals which is best will be known only as general intelligence is diffused, and as the intelligent are led to inquire and to judge. Even the contentions among Christians themselves tend to this result, because if there be any truth in the Gospel, it will eventually come out of these controversies The people of these United States are singularly blessed that no regal or sacerdotal power, and no political authority, presents any obstacle to free inquiry. The tongue, the pen, and the press, together with free discussion and free speech, will bring about the true philosophy and practice, whatever that may be found to be.

A NOBLE LIFE.

Exertion is the price of a noble life. The pursuit of a noble object adorns, ennobles, and vivifies life. Without definite aim, life is like a rudderless ship, drifting about between life and death, and entirely at the mercy of the waves. While one with folded arms waits for future opportunities, another makes the meanest occurrences subservient to a golden result. One labors to find something to do; the other labors to do something. When the Alps intercepted his line of march, Napoleon said, "There shall be no Alps." When difficulties from poverty, and difficulties from the opposition of friends beset him, Franklin resolutely determined there should be no difficulties. Greatness has in its vocabulary no such word as fail. It will work; it must succeed. Happy is he who at the sunset of life can recall the years that have gone swift-footed by, without bringing before him a fearful array of squandered opportunities.

ACTIONS.

The important object that bears upon society, refers itself to the actions of men. Stephen Girard was perhaps as irreproachable in his habits as the generality of his species, and did much good. Yet he has been reproached for his opinions. The legitimate inquiry of society ought to have reference only to our conduct. Is he sober and industrious? Is he a good husband, a good father, an exemplary, upright citizen? Is he honest and square in his dealings? There are few of us that live up to the standard here indicated. It is pleasant, however, to feel and know that we have reached that point of improvement where we have found out that he who is all these, stands not in need of clerical interposition to give him a passport to heaven. We have a heaven on earth, in that peace of mind, the reward of virtue.

When, therefore, the religionists of the day come to compare notes with us, where do we differ? We do not believe, they say. True, we do not believe in professions, in doctrines, in creeds. These are not of God; they are of man: they are the inventions of designing men, who would live upon the credulity of their fellow-men, instead of the exercise of that labor which they denounce as a curse. We would not be understood to charge these designs upon those who now believe and act conscientiously. This is not our intention. We believe they are sincere, and we only ask them to extend the same charity to us. The great concern of mankind is charity.

RIGHTS.

All just governments originate with the people. With respect to religious and political rights, we are all born equal. "One half of mankind (as the Democratic Jefferson said) "are not born with saddles on their backs, and the other half born booted and spurred, ready to ride them by the grace of God." Might can never make that right which is not right in itself. There are certain inalienable rights of which no man can be deprived — unless forfeited by crime — without violating a natural and fundamental principle of justice. Of these are the rights of conscience. We have the same natural right to entertain, to express, and to disseminate our Infidel opinions, that our Christian neighbor has to promulgate and advocate his. And if all our neighbors should be of one opinion, and we alone should differ with them, the case, as it respects rights, is not at all altered. They would have the *power*, but they would have no more *right* to injure us than we should have to injure them.

Upon the very same principle, a majority of the people in this commonwealth, however great that majority might be, would have no more natural right, if so disposed, to make and put in force any law which should injure a single individual of the state, on account of his religious sentiments, or the open profession of them, than they would to take an innocent man's life.

RELIGION AND COMMON SENSE.

We hear a great deal about "pure religion," and the phrase seems to be an admission that all religion is not pure, which is no doubt the fact; but what quality of religion is genuine, or who possess it, may be difficult to decide. And even if we knew, how much better off should we be? For what is religion, in itself considered, and separate from morality, to which it has no just or proper claim? It is a system of faith in, and worship of, supernatural agencies and beings. That is about all there is of it, when summed up in brief. It may exist, no doubt, in the character of a good man, but it is no proof of goodness in the individual, nor that he is laboring for the welfare of humanity. It is only, as we have said, a system of faith and worship having reference to the supernatural. That is religion, and all that rightly belongs to it. We fail to see wherein it can be of any benefit to this world; and as for another, it is not settled yet whether there is one.

Now in order to have a system that is useful and practical, it ought not to consist in unmeaning phrases, forms, and ceremonies, but in the unceasing practice of promoting the happiness of every human being, without regard to sex, party, country, or color — and confine its labors entirely to this world, depending on knowledge rather than faith, and human efforts instead of prayers to a supernatural Deity. This is a common-sense system or philosophy, and one in which there are no metaphysical difficulties or mystery, and which every child even, who is properly educated, will be taught to practise through life — and which he will necessarily practise, as no incentive to injure his fellow-man will then exist, such as form an inherent and essential part of the present order of society. Under the common-sense system to which we allude, there would not be the slightest pretext for keeping up those holy bugbears which are supposed by many Christians to be so indispensable at present to control the vicious inclinations of human beings, such as avenging Gods, devils, priestly prayers, and denunciations; but mankind will be governed by reason, and learn their duty by obeying the laws of Nature, which are the only true guides.

SCIENCE AND RELIGION.

It is generally agreed, we believe, that the human race has made great progress in the arts and sciences, and it seems equally plain and self-evident that the fact excites no fear or alarm. We nowhere find, in civilized nations, that the people complain because they are superior, in regard to invention and discovery, to their ancestors who preceded them. On the contrary, they exult at the beneficial change, and joyfully " accept the situation." They congratulate themselves on the material improvement everywhere visible, and the man who at this day should sigh for the return of the ancient age, when art and science were almost unknown, would be considered as an anomaly indeed, if not bereft of his senses. He would be thought to be one of those unfortunate people who prefer to grope their way in blindness and ignorance, as was the fate of the masses of mankind before the invention of the printing-press and the mariner's compass. And if mankind are not disturbed at their physical improvement over the past, so neither are they, in this respect, in regard to the future. If in the coming generations, our descendants shall be able to travel in safety a hundred miles an hour on the railroads, or sail in the air about the country in balloon-ships, or walk on the water as on the land, or by some " elixir of life " prolong existence to five hundred years, supposing these things possible and probable, they give no uneasiness in prospect, nor will they if realized. Somehow, mankind have no apprehension of danger from physical discoveries in any of the departments of science, but seem to rest satisfied with the conviction that it is all for the best, and thus it is that in this particular, at least, the most intelligent Christians and all heretics are united, as it were, on a common ground.

But when we come to " religion," as it is called, the whole scene changes. Here there is no progress, nor can there be in the nature of the case, and it is sinful and wicked to allow of any. Religion is said to be divine, and of course it is a finality, for it includes everything in its especial department, and cannot possibly be improved upon in any degree whatever, therefore it is perfect, and progress where there is perfection is entirely superfluous, unnecessary, and out of the question. Yet (and here is the crowning absurdity), this standard of moral truth and duty called religion, was proclaimed eighteen hundred years ago, among an ignorant people in an obscure corner of the earth, and it is in tended for, and is strictly applicable to, all mankind in all ages to come, as long as time shall last, for as it came from God, mortal man can never improve upon it! Such is the nature of religion, as defined by its teachers. It is perfect all through, and consequently needs not and cannot have any improvement. But mankind make progress in everything else? Undoubtedly, and they glory in the fact; yet in religion, the motto has always been, since its birth, and is now, " Keep as you are ; remove not the ancient landmarks of our faith and worship, or the moral world will tumble into ruins." This, in substance, has been the cry of religion for the last two thousand years, nearly, and when from time to time during this long period men have appeared in Europe and opposed this religion on the ground that it was imperfect and might be improved, they were denounced as " Infidels," enemies, and burnt to death. No other course could have been pursued with them under the circumstances. They opposed a religion which claims to be Divine, and was so regarded, and as their opposition was considered to be the unpardonable sin, they were persecuted and put to death in honor of the church and for the glory of God. Their punishment as unavoidably grew out of religion, as effect flows from cause, and herein is involved the radical, intrinsic, inherent, or the fundamental error which has always made and always will make religion a hindrance and a stumbling-block in the path of progress; namely, it forbids improvement. "If any man preach any other Gospel than this, let him be accursed." Here, in this admonition of a New Testament Apostle, we have the spirit which has always characterized religion, and rendered it an injury rather than a blessing to mankind. Established in an age of ignorance and superstition, and presuming to be Divine or perfect, religion has necessarily been a clog or barrier to mental improvement; for arrogating to itself perfection at the start, it had nothing to learn, because it claimed to know everything when it commenced. But this is folly, as the knowledge possessed to-day by mankind has been obtained by long and patient study, observation, and experience, and therefore it is not less absurd to teach that Adam and Eve were born or created a full-grown man and woman, than it is to claim that a religion of eighteen centuries ago cannot be improved upon, but is exactly fitted for the moral and intellectual condition of the race as long as it shall exist. With just as much propriety might it be maintained, that the clothes of the infant are adapted to the growth and size of the man, or that the little amount of knowledge generally possessed in ancient times, is all that mankind will ever require in the present and future. The poor simpleton of a courtier whom we used to read of in the story books, who thought in his vanity that he could chain the waves, was no more out in his reckoning than those Christians who vainly attempt to fasten a padlock upon the human mind, and keep it eternally in one position. It cannot be done. The mind will sooner or later throw off its trammels, for it is always restless and active, and this being its nature, there can be no finality to any subject of thought, as every generation will have its own views upon it. Hence it is that the Christian religion, proclaimed in Judea eighteen centuries ago, has been as unavoidably improved as the notions of science that prevailed at that time, and in these days the improvement of the former is greatly accelerated. PROGRESS is the standard under which the world is now marching, and religion, as well as science and government, must "fall in" or "go under."

THOUGHTS ON LIFE AND DEATH.

One of the leading doctrines of the Christian Religion is, as a prayer for the sick expresses it, " to fit and prepare for death." Now there is no reasonable objection, when a person is near his final hour, to making his last moments as easy, quiet, and peaceful as possible, in order that the sufferer may pass off to his rest in as comfortable a manner as the kind offices of friends can devise. And if to some people this desirable effect can be brought about by prayer, it might be used on about the same principle as physicians give an anodyne, to tranquilize the nerves. The doctor does not expect to accomplish a cure when he sees recovery impossible, and therefore he turns his attention towards rendering the last moments of his patient as quiet and painless as medical skill and experience can suggest. The motive is prompted by kindness, and so everybody who possesses this feeling, approves of the course of the doctor in such cases. On the same principle and for the same purpose, prayer might be beneficial; and if it can be, there is no more that is unreasonable, perhaps, as far as the sick man is concerned, in praying for him, than there is in assuaging his mortal pains with some oblivious opiate. We should always be ready and willing to do any act which benefits our fellow-men, when the motive for the action is dictated by kindness and benevolence, and when it involves no surrender of what we regard to be true.

The great objection, however, to prayer in the Christian sense as a preparation for death, consists in the fact that it is very apt to be viewed as a substitute or as an equivalent for a good and useful life. This is a great and ruinous error, and one that seems to be sanctioned by the New Testament itself, in its familiar examples of "the eleventh hour" and the death of "the penitent thief on the cross." The only inference from this kind of teaching is, that a bad life may be atoned for by a little contrition or sorrow just before death. As well might the farmer in autumn of the year expect to gather a crop from a field he had never tilled, as a transgressor through life expect to become a good and virtuous man on his deathbed, by a little sorrow or repentance over a long and criminal course of conduct. It is a monstrous absurdity, and the only influence it can have is to increase crime, rather than diminish it.

And these reflections lead us to see the utter folly of attaching any importance to death under such circumstances; nor is it a true test, in any case whatever, that the life has been uniformly correct and upright. It may, and no doubt does happen that a man's last hours, if he have mind enough left to think at all, will prove the sincerity with which he holds his opinions, whatever they may be; but this is no proof that his life has been morally good.

It is character, alone, that makes the right kind of a man, and character is acquired only by unexceptionable conduct in our everyday life and intercourse with one another, and not in the solitude and privacy of a sick-chamber, when, our work done and our mission ended, we lay ourselves down to die. So that the Christian doctrine, "*After* death comes the judgment," is not by any means of as much consequence as the judgment which is passed on a man's character BEFORE his death.

Besides, sickness is not a proper time to form an estimate of conduct or mind either. As well judge of the strength and completeness of a building when its timbers and walls are tumbling to the ground, as of the mental and physical condition of the man, who, amid the nausea of medicine and the spasms of dissolving nature, is but a mere wreck, and "nothing is but what is not." From all such sickly fancies, engendered by religion, we turn to the teachings of Nature and Reason, and we learn from them that if we would form a true estimate of mankind, we must consider their peculiarities or characters when in a state of health and action. There can be no error or mistake in this course, for here we judge the tree by the fruit. Prayers and professions are only breath, and in themselves considered are of no account; but a good life is always pure gold, and like that, never fails to be appreciated.

Not to deathbeds, then, are we to look for evidences of goodness in any man, but to his life, and to that alone; and if he has been in his dealings honest, truthful, moral, just, and kind, his life has been in the right, though he may never have made a prayer, nor attended a church, nor read a chapter of the Bible. In religion, these ceremonies are indispensable; but as they are not inherent proofs of goodness, it follows that what mankind most need for their improvement and happiness is not religion but moral character. Religion has reference to another world, of which no one knows anything; morality relates wholly to the duties which a man owes to himself and his fellowmen here in this life — and these duties can be known and practised. There is, therefore, as much difference between morality and religion, as the governing rules or guides of conduct, as there is between the truthful principles of Reason, and the fanciful vagaries of a blind superstition.

FOLLOW THE LIGHT OF EVIDENCE.

Education, passion, and external circumstances have a powerful influence in bewildering the minds of honest and well-intentioned individuals. But however gaudily an hypothesis may be dressed, an inquirer after truth ought not for a moment to be dazzled by the meretricious glitter. "He should (as the Rev. Dr. Chalmers observes in his *Evidences of Christianity*) be prepared to FOLLOW THE LIGHT OF EVIDENCE, though it may lead him to conclusions the most painful and melancholy; he should train his mind to all the hardihood of abstract and unfeeling intelligence; he should give up everything to the supremacy of argument, and be able to renounce without a sigh, all the tenderest prepossessions of infancy, the moment the truth demands of him the sacrifice.

Now, keeping this good advice in mind, let us look for a few moments at Nature, or the Material Universe, as the uncaused, the self-existent being or state, and contrast it with the opposite or the spiritual idea, in order that we may discover which of the two is the more philosophical. Take for illustration, a watch: we infer from its peculiar structure and purpose that it had a maker; experience tells us that its maker must have been an intelligent being, whom we term man. We then find that man is a much more complicated machine than a watch, and our next inquiry is, *Who made man?* Here experience deserts us. We see a regular succession of men and women, but no one can show us their origin. Then, as experience is no guide in this matter, we endeavor to solve the question by the help of analogy. But here we are precisely as much in the dark as ever: for though we infer that machinery of a kind quite new to us, is made by a machinist, yet we have never seen any animal created, and therefore have no good ground to infer a creator. Still, as it was evident that there were powers in Nature with which mankind were unacquainted, and which in the rude periods of society appeared to be wielded by invisible but capricious hands, the notion of an intelligent but an incomprehensible being arose; and thus, perhaps, as Lucretius says, "Fear first made Gods in the world."

This notion, thus originating, and afterwards so successfully propagated in so many shapes and by so many means, acquired a firm footing on the earth, and all who were bold enough to question the received dogmas of the priests and churches were persecuted as vile unbelievers. We have at last arrived then, at the popular reason for a belief in a Deity, though it is impossible to find any agreement among the various sects in the different religions in the world respecting him, except that he is entirely incomprehensible. If you admit that this Deity made man and the universe, but venture to inquire into the origin of *his* existence, you are directly told that he is an uncaused, self-existent, and eternal being, omnipresent, omnipotent, immutable, and infinitely wise and benevolent. Now an intelligent inquirer having this theory before him, perceives its complete variance with facts and experience, and rejects it. He sees no reason for admitting more causes than were necessary to produce the effects observed, and not being able to see the impression of any other hand in Nature than matter and motion, rejects what he considers as superfluous. The believer says, mankind or the universe cannot have existed without a cause, but he says that the cause of mankind and the universe requires no cause. This uncaused first cause, he says is infinitely superior to the universe of matter, but acknowledges it to be quite incomprehensible. He also allows that the essence of matter is quite as incomprehensible as the nature of the Deity, but he decides without hesitation, that the one requires a cause, and the other no cause for its existence.

The unbeliever, guided solely by experience and analogy, looks upon matter as eternally existing, for he can find no evidence of its commencement. He invests it with no attributes which contradict acknowledged facts, and so long as he finds disorder, vice, and misery making up so large a portion of the ingredients in the world, he cannot infer infinite power, wisdom, and benevolence to be among its attributes. He cannot perceive any incongruity in ascribing to matter the powers and qualities of which he finds it possessed, nor can he see the necessity of deriving those powers and qualities from another being, who can neither be seen, heard, felt, nor understood; is cognizable by no one sense; and by those who talk most loudly about him is declared to be totally incomprehensible even to themselves. Who, then, is it, ought to be charged with being shallow and unphilosophical? He who is guided by experience and analogy; or he who deserts those safe and certain paths, and roams into the regions of conjecture, and dogmatically demands the credence of his fellow-men to *the narrations of his own fancy?*

WHAT IS TRUTH?

We are told in the New Testament, that, at the trial of Jesus, Pilate asked the question, " *What is Truth?* " But, if we remember the record correctly, he did not wait, or rather did not seek for an answer. And so it has been from that day to this, mankind ask the same question as did Pilate, and, like him, are too careless, indifferent, or too much in a hurry to discover the proper answer. They are in the habit of depending on others for their opinions, and hence the small amount, comparatively, of genuine free thought and mental independence. In all ages of the world, and even now to a considerable extent, certain teachers spring up with a " Lo here and lo there, I am right, follow me," and the multitude take them at their word and " fall into line." We see this fact illustrated in the history of the Catholic Church and the swarming myriads of devotees that crowd her portals. The Protestant Church shows more disintegration or independence, but this is not owing to any intrinsic merit of her own, but wholly to the exercise of the right of private judgment, which is an Infidel rather than a Christian principle. And if so, it goes to prove — what every observing man knows to be a demonstrated fact — that just in proportion as Christianity becomes Infidelized, does it become sensible, liberal, practical, human, natural, and useful. And this also proves another important fact; namely, that Christianity is not needed.

What is wanted is, not any kind of religion that ever was or is now taught. The world has had enough of it, and altogether too much. Let it all go to speedy oblivion, bag and baggage, for it has been "weighed in the balance (for thousands of years) and found wanting." But what do you propose to give as a substitute? asks a religious inquirer. TRUTH. And what is that? A conformity to fact or reality; or, as Frances Wright used to express the same idea, truth is knowledge, and knowledge "signifies things known," and furthermore, " where there are no things to be known, there can be no knowledge." We accept this doctrine as thoroughly correct, and it comprises what we mean by Infidelity and Atheism. Applied to science, it tells us that every science, that is, every branch of knowledge, is compounded of certain facts, of which our sensations furnish the evidence. Where no such evidence is supplied; we are without data; we are without first premises; and when, without these, we attempt to build up a science, we do as those do who raise edifices without foundations. And what do such architects or builders construct? Castles in the air.

Now if we have given a correct idea of the

nature of truth, and the basis of all genuine or real science, let us look a moment at the course we should pursue in order to arrive at truth. We must be bold, independent, and fearless at the start, be inquirers and investigators of the most radical or thorough description, examining fully and freely every doctrine, and submitting it to the tribunal of reason for acceptance or rejection. There are people who say this is dangerous ground. They are blind guides, let them not be trusted. It is knowledge that we are in pursuit of, and that is not dangerous, or something of which we are to be afraid. What is the danger of truth? Or where is the danger of fact? Error and ignorance are, indeed, full of danger. They fill our imagination with terrors; they place us at the mercy of every external circumstance; they incapacitate us for our duties as members of the human family, for happiness as sentient beings, and for improvement as reasonable beings. This illusion, then, that in our inquiries we can go "too fast and too far" must be discarded. We must understand, therefore, what knowledge is, and when we have attained it we shall clearly perceive that it regards all equally; that truth or fact is the same thing for all human kind; that there are not truths for the rich and truths for the poor; truths for men and truths for women; but that there are simply truths; that is, facts, which all who open their eyes and their ears and their understandings can perceive. There is no mystery in these facts; there is no witchcraft in knowledge. Science is not a trick, nor a puzzle; the philosopher is not a conjurer, the observer of Nature who envelopes his discoveries in mysteries, either knows less than he pretends, or feels interested in withholding his knowledge; and the teacher whose lessons are difficult of comprehension is either clumsy or he is ignorant.

MAN.

"The proper study of mankind is man."

We agree with the famous poet, that " The proper study of mankind is man." He is the highest object as it regards his physical, intellectual, or religious character; presents the greatest variety in operation, and holds forth the most boundless field of speculation as it regards the future.

1. In his physical constitution he is above all other animals. Comparative anatomy, which is brought in only to illustrate the beauty and elegancy of his form, abundantly confirms our position. No skeleton can be compared to his. The sinews, skin, muscles, tissues, formation, habits, and movements of no class of beings now known can vie with him. Others are stronger, more swift, less affected by change of climate, season, food, drink, and surfeit; but as a whole he stands preeminent.

2. In his intellectual constitution, likewise,

there is no comparison. He improves upon disappointment and defeat. He combines the wisdom of ages. All the master-spirits of the world leave the concentrated light and energy of their discoveries spread upon his mind. Poets, historians, sculptors, painters, patriots and philanthropists, though they have passed away, live in his memory and breathe with his expiration. Standing on the earth, whirled at the rate of more than a million and a half miles a day in its course around the sun and all the universe in twenty-four hours coursing above it, he has been enabled in the exercise of mind to admeasure its course, weigh its materia, poise the sun, and to determine the nearest positive approach it can ever make to the nearest fixed star. He has, untaught but by himself, been enabled to demonstrate that the universe is infinite. Thus a finite being arrives at infinity! But how? By intellect. Can any being or class of beings do more?

3. In his religious or superstitious character, he is wonderful. He has peopled the past, present and future. He has united time and eternity. He has thrown the creation of an eternal reality over the regions of fancy and imagination. Gods, devils, heaven, and hell, the thunders of omnipotence and the lightning of omniscience are at his command. Clouds, storm, and tempest; light, beauty, and sublimity are his playthings. He dashes, mingles, separates, and convolves to suit

his ends. His body streaks the earth or sweeps the ocean with a velocity too great to suffer his features to be recognized, but his mind, in its secret and impetuous course, outstrips the lightning, and not infrequently in the frail body of some Shakespeare and Newton claims ubiquity with all intellects or with all worlds. If we come to the variety of his operations, there is no angle at which he cannot strike, no complex combination of numbers which he cannot solve, no climate that he cannot breathe, no mechanism which he cannot construct. Birds, beast, fish, insects, all yield to him. He combines the varied operation of all. He rises infinitely above them. The ocean is his playground and the mountain his monument. He combines all combination and evolves all evolution.

But what of his future destination? The inventive genius of the nineteenth century is but the slumber and dream of ages. Who can tell what physical and intellectual energies he may not evolve? If he can now cause light to paint the living image, who can deny that it is in the compass of his inventive power to concentrate mind itself and give it "a local habitation and a name." Thus on all these points in his physical constitution, his intellectual energies, his superstitious devices, the variety of his operations and his future promise, he as an object of wonder rises above all others. " The proper study of mankind is man." It is so in another point of view, and that especially adverted to by the poet. To an individual, no other study is so important. No art, skill, or science will avail him if ignorant of mankind. He is circumvented by the artful and ruined by the unjust. He may be compared to a world destitute of repulsive power and doomed to be lost in the magnitude of some inferior orb without it.

WHAT HUMANITY NEEDS.

According to the religious teachers everywhere to be met with, this world would hardly be fit to live in were it not for Christianity. Now if this be really the case, we Infidels and Atheists are certainly engaged in a bad work, for we are opposing the greatest blessing that humanity possesses and can have. But we are not yet prepared to accept this conclusion, and in the remarks which follow we will endeavor to give briefly a few of the reasons why, in our opinion, mankind can have a far better guide, counsellor, and director than religion, as generally understood, or that form of superstition known as Christianity.

We start, then, with the idea, which seems to us self-evidently true, that, as a general rule, ignorance is the great cause of human errors, contentions, strife, trouble, and misconduct, — and knowledge is the remedy. As a general principle, this is correct, we think. Mankind, not being bad by nature, and every one without exception, perhaps, being in pursuit of happiness, how is it that so many of our race make such terrible mistakes, and bring upon themselves misery, degradation, wretchedness, hatred, and crime? Are these afflictions desirable or from choice? Does any man, woman or child sincerely want them and strive to secure them? Most certainly not, if they are of sane mind. Then, why are these calamities so common on every hand? Because of ignorance, or because of not knowing how to live properly or happily *in this world*. If anybody can think of any better reason, he will please to send it to us by telegraph, or post haste. It cannot come too quick, for if we are in error we wish to know " that better way."

We believe, however, that we state the true cause and cure of human ills and woes, when we say that ignorance is the cause, and knowledge, the cure. Here we have the bane and the antidote; the disease and the panacea. Knowledge, or a clear and certain perception of truth or fact as it exists in Nature and ourselves; an understanding of natural and organic laws, and of our individual duties, together with those that we owe to one another and to society; in a word, an education or a training that shall make mankind moral, just, kind, useful, practical, and secular in all things, is what is needed to start our race on the right track, to keep it there, and to produce the greatest amount of happiness, improvement, and utility of which human beings are susceptible.

But religion, which is founded in ignorance and superstition, cannot from its very nature be adapted to benefit humanity, and if we may credit its history, it never did. Nor do we see why it should. Its very essence is bigotry and persecution; it opposes inquiry, science, progress; makes duty and virtue consist in the belief and support of irrational or useless sectarian dogmas, and finally sets up the boast that its "kingdom is not of this world." For these and many other reasons that might be urged, the Christian religion is not adapted to human beings on earth, whatever it may do for them in "Heaven," if there be one.

SECTARIAN SCHOOLS.

If state and church were united in this country, the Government might consistently support these schools; but as such is not the case, it cannot. Then again, all classes are taxed to sustain common schools; — Infidels, Spiritualists, Free Religionists, Jews, and the Nothingarians, as well as Protestants and Catholics. But the two latter classes arrogantly claim that *they* must manage in this matter, as though they were the only supporters of the schools, and had the exclusive right to dictate their management. Accordingly, the

Protestants say that the Bible must be kept in the schools, and they seem to expect that all the other parties named must acquiesce in this decision, and keep on paying their taxes as usual for the maintenance of these institutions. The Catholics on the other hand say as arrogantly, that the Protestant Bible must be taken out of the schools, but they give the public to understand that theirs must be put in, to take its place, else the schools must be broken up. This is about the way that the dispute stands at present. It is a quarrel as to which Bible (St James's or the Douay version) is to have the preference in the schools, and these belligerent Christians appear to entertain the idea that we outsiders will support either party that happens to gain the ascendency. It is "rule or ruin" with both of them, and consequently the preservation of the schools on an anti-sectarian basis rests wholly with Liberals. On any other basis, the schools must necessarily suffer in value, if not eventually become perverted from their original useful object.

Now as our government is not religious, it is plain that the common schools, supported by common taxation, should be devoted to secular teaching and to nothing else. There can be no other just and equal plan, because if the Protestant and Catholic may introduce their Bibles into the schools to be read by the scholars, then the Infidel may bring in Voltaire's writings, and the Spiritualist, those of Andrew Jackson Davis. All four classes pay taxes to maintain the schools, and therefore are equally entitled, by right and justice, to a voice in their management. But as secularism is the only subject on which people do not quarrel, let *that* be the basis of the public schools, and their foundation is on a rock. Build them on sectarianism, or the Bible, and they rest on sand.

INDIVIDUALITY.

When a man discovers what he believes to be an error in science, in art, in politics, in religion, or in anything else that in any way affects or influences humanity, either individually or collectively, it is his manifest duty to correct it, if he can, and administer a preventive, if possible, that will act as a safeguard against its recurrence in the future.

A man's intellect is his own individual kingdom, over which he reigns supreme. It is his intellect, and his intellect alone, that enables him to assert and maintain his individuality. So long as he relies on his own individual powers of ratiocination as his best and surest guide in all the discharge of the various duties of life, he stands forth among the people, a bright and shining example of individual existence and individual responsibility. But the moment he abandons his self-reliance, and depends for his opinions and ideas, and almost his intellectual existence, upon the opinions and ideas of others, he loses his personal identity and becomes an intellectual parasite, stealing from others the wealth they have labored to procure, and which he is too lazy to work for.

It is in this condition of abandoned self-reliance that we find the great mass of the people in respect to religion. They do not seem to take a sufficient amount of interest in religion, to give the matter a personal investigation. They are content to have their ministers do their religious thinking, and form their religious opinions for them, while they arrange themselves comfortably among their cushions, and lazily bask in the sunshine of a delusive hope. This saves them a deal of trouble, and relieves them of a great responsibility; for in the event of their being right, there *is* no responsibility.

But should they be wrong, the responsibility rests with crushing weight upon their ministerial guide who has blinded their eyes, and succeeded in leading them, through the promises of a blissful hereafter, into the deceptive sloughs and bogs of a supernatural religion.

SUNDAY.

It is often said that Infidels wish to destroy Sunday, but this is not correct; they would make it far more useful and profitable. This is all the change they propose, and it cannot truly be argued that this is any opposition to the day itself. They would remove from it the superstition and the bigotry which have so long been connected with it; they would use it to promote goodness, for humanity, for science, for letters, for society. They would not abuse it by impudent license on the one hand, nor by slavish superstition on the other. We can easily escape the evils which come of the old abuse; can make the Sunday ten times more valuable than it is now; can employ it for all the highest interests of mankind, and fear no reaction into libertinism.

The Sunday is made for man, as are all other days, not man for Sunday. Let us use it, then, not consuming its hours in a Jewish observance; not devote it to the lower necessities of life, but the higher; not squander it in idleness, sloth, frivolity, or sleep; let us use it for the body's rest, and for the mind's improvement. The Sunday has come down to us from our ancestors as a day to be devoted to the highest interests of man. It has done good service, no doubt, for them and for us. But it has come down accompanied with superstition, which robs it of half its value. It is easy for the present generation to make the day far more profitable to themselves than it ever was to their fathers; easy to divest it of all bigotry, to free it from all oldness of the letter; easy to leave it for posterity, an institution which shall bless them for many ages to come; or it is easy to bind on their necks unnatural restraints; to impose on their conscience and understanding absurdities that at last they must repel with scorn and contempt.

INFIDELITY.

As much as Infidelity is scouted and opposed, it is a curious fact that every great revolution strengthens Infidelity and weakens the church. Every circumstance that sets men to thinking, creates Infidels; and every attempt to improve the condition of any large class of the community, whether they are borne down by vice or by oppression, is sure to meet with such opposition from the church, that reformers in fighting for these good works are obliged to fight the church into the bargain. The temperance reformers have been obliged to fight the church in carrying on their good work; other social reformers are obliged to do the same; and so are the Democrats, at least all of the party who are true to the principles which they profess. All genuine philanthropists, all genuine reformers, therefore, are obliged to fight the church, while contending for their good works; and Infidelity gains new ground by being always on the side of reform. But whatever is proscriptive and intolerant the church defends.

This is the state of things, and it shows that so intimately connected is religion with all established laws, customs, and institutions, that no innovation can be attempted for the removal of any social evil, without giving more offence to the church than to any other body of men. At the same time the church claims to be the great moral and social physician, whose spiritual panacea is the only remedy for the ills and woes of life. Yet it is notorious that when any practical reform is to be commenced, it has to be undertaken outside of the church and by men whom the church condemns as Infidels, everybody being considered as an Infidel by the church, who steps out of her old and beaten track.

In short, it is self-evident to every observer that the church and priesthood have always been the greatest obstacles in existence to all moral and intellectual progress; and we may set it down as certain, that only in proportion as they are deprived of power and influence, can the condition of mankind be ameliorated. We consider all Infidels, therefore, as pioneers in the important work of universal redemption, for they are engaged in the task of removing the chief obstacle to political and moral improvement.

THE INTELLECTUAL FACULTIES.

They are much mistaken, who think that it is useless to attempt instructing ourselves at an advanced period of life. Such truths as we may have remained ignorant of during our earlier years, may still sometimes shed a benign influence over the closing scene of our existence.

All we have to do, is to occupy our intellectual faculties in calculating justly our wants; to employ our capabilities with greatest effect in obtaining their gratification; and, finally, we should always submit ourselves to the necessity of our nature and the inevitable conditions of our brief organization and consciousness.

A person, in the maturity of reason, doubts; in disease, his prejudices revive. Priests then exult, terming his former doubts pretence or audacity; they pretend to consider dereliction of mind, by sickness or dotage, the time for sound and deliberate thinking. How common a case is this, and yet it is as unwise as to judge of the strength of a building when its timbers are falling to the ground. Reason tells us that when the mind is enfeebled, the prejudices of infancy may recur, and strength may give place to weakness and decay; but a man in the maturity of his intellect and in good physical health, with his mind well established in the principles of truth, and aware of the realities of eternal Nature, will not be likely to turn fanatic under any circumstances.

FREEDOM OF OPINION.

No man should be blamed, injured, or molested on account of his opinions, whether right or wrong, on any subject. For we always suppose our own opinions to be right, or we should renounce them. And with respect to belief, every one must be the judge for himself. A person may be blamable for so conceited, so bigoted an attachment to his own opinions, as not to hear, and reasonably weigh, all the reasons, proofs, and arguments against them. Every one is justly blamable, and answerable to himself, for erroneous opinions conceived or retained for want of such impartial examination as his situation enables him to use, or from an obstinate conviction of their infallibility. And this is all the blame that can reasonably be attached to any one on account of his belief, because the opinions of men are above their control.

Every one comes to a conclusion on any given subject, when a certain weight of evidence has been received, enough to produce conviction on his mind; although perhaps to another individual whose mind is differently constituted, the same evidence is quite insufficient. So that one may believe, and another disbelieve the same thing, having the same evidence, and both be equally sincere and guiltless. Our opinions are not subject to our will. We cannot believe and disbelieve as we please. The only effect, therefore, which laws, punishments, penalties, and disabilities can possibly have, is to render it prudent for individuals, if they entertain unpopular or unlawful belief, to conceal it, and — in self-defence and against their own will — to cover themselves in the garb of hypocrisy.

PROTESTANTS — CATHOLICS.

There is a difference between these sects as regards their attitude towards the all-important Right of Private Judgment. Not that the former admit it in its fulness or entirety, but they come nearer to it than the latter, at least theoretically, and hence we prefer the Protestants to Catholics. Then again, the very nature of Protestantism, (or protest against an infallible church,) tends to division, disintegration, and individuality, which accounts for its almost numberless sects, showing that there is no real bond of union between them. Once tell men they have a right to think, even partially, and they will surely differ in opinion.

We see this fact illustrated in the career of Protestantism. Its doctrines of two hundred years ago are greatly modified or nearly obsolete in its church to-day, and this goes to prove that before another century is finished, Protestantism will then be among the things that were, or swallowed up in Liberalism, towards which it is drifting. So that the struggle for Free Thought, now, and in the future, will not be so much between Liberals and Protestants, as between Liberals and Catholics, and in this struggle, the Liberals are destined to win, unless the human mind retrogrades into the Dark Ages, and of that there is no probability. "Revolutions never go backwards."

MORAL INFLUENCE.

The influence of a good example is far reaching; for our experience and conflicts with the world lead us at times to indulge misanthropic sentiments, and charge all men with selfish and impure motives. The play of pride, prejudice, and passion, and the eagerness manifested by the great majority of men to advance their own interests, often at the expense of others, and in violation of the Golden Rule, cause us to look with suspicion on the best intents of others. Arrogance, hypocrisy, treachery, and violence, every day outrage justice, till we are almost disposed to distrust human nature, and become discouraged.

But amid all that is sad and disheartening in this busy, noisy world, now and then there is presented to us a life of such uniform virtue, that we recognize in it a character that brings hope for the perfect development and ultimate regeneration of our race. Such characters are very precious, and such examples should be held up to the world for its admiration and imitation; they should be snatched from oblivion and treasured in the hearts and thoughts of all who are in process of forming habits and character.

RELIGION IN THE PUBLIC SCHOOLS.

An institution maintained by the taxes of the entire community — not only by Christians, but by Liberals, Spiritualists, and Free-thinkers as well — should not be partial, exclusive, or favor one portion of taxpayers more than another. This is equal rights; it is "even-handed justice," and it should be exercised in regard to the public schools not less than in other institutions sustained by the people at large. But this democratic principle is not now recognized in the management of the public schools of Boston, and never was, so far as we can learn.

They are, and always have been Christian — yet the Liberals, Spiritualists, Free-thinkers, and Nothingarians are compelled by law to pay taxes to support schools for teaching a religion in which these classes do not believe! This is the plain, unvarnished truth, but we are told every hour that here in Massachusetts there is no mental coercion; that we have no established religion and no union of Church and State! This kind of talk is idle, and worse, for it is fraud and deception. The reading-books used in the public schools of this city, are, and always have been permeated by *Christianity*, and hence are sectarian in their teaching.

FORMATION OF OPINIONS.

All men are born equal with regard to the formation of opinions; by nature they are allowed the free exercise of their own judgments, equality in investigating, considering, and determining upon all subjects. Yet, notwithstanding this truth will be universally admitted (in the abstract), it seems to be generally disregarded in the application to religion. Hence it is common to hear the remark, by those who denounce innovations upon the popular religious belief, that opinions ought to be governed by the general sentiment.

But this course, besides directly tending to destroy all freedom of conscience, would perpetuate the superstition and ignorance which it is desirable to remove, and prevent the diffusion of the knowledge which all deem necessary and desire to see progressive. We should not adopt opinions merely because they are popular; if the error is general, so much the greater should be the exertion to destroy it. If, by ignorance or by some blind fanaticism, the generality of mankind have been deceived into error must a man for the sake of popularity join in the concert of deception, and the honest sentiments of his mind remain lost and inactive?

If the opinions of mankind are to remain fixed, when their only claims to belief are antiquity and universality, through fear of encountering opposition or of being unpopular, what advance or improvement could we expect in any knowledge of any kind? Oppose the liberty of thought, and you retard the progress of knowledge; encourage investigation, and a new era arises; knowledge of all kinds advances with rapid strides, and man becomes, as it were, a new creature.

A CHURCH.

The object of a church is to teach doctrines having reference to another world in another state of being; and even if this plan does some good, it is of doubtful tendency, on the whole, for it begins, as it were, at the wrong end Admitting a future world in which mankind are to live after they have got through with this, what will give them the best preparation for that existence? Evidently to instruct them in the laws of their physical, moral, and mental nature, and in addition, to place them as far as possible in those favorable circumstances which promote health, happiness, and longevity. These things are unquestionably of the first importance in this life, and indispensable, we should suppose, to our well-being in the next, if there is to be such an arrangement in reserve for us, on the same principle, it would seem, that in order to live properly to-morrow, we must know how to live properly to-day.

The whole question is involved in the manner of living, not in religious faith, professions, nor building churches, but in supplying natural wants in a rational and practical mode, so as to remove inducements or temptations to vice and crime. Ignorance and poverty lead to misconduct and wretchedness, as every observing person is well aware; and hence the remedy for them does not consist in lavishing millions on gorgeous tabernacles, but in improving the bad social condition in which the poor and ignorant are placed.

BLIND FAITH.

If blind faith had no other tendency than that of leading to the stability of virtue and its consequent happiness, it ought to be tolerated whether true or false. The grand object of life is to augment the sum of human enjoyment on earth, and whatever tends to that end is decidedly good, and therefore demands the support of all well-meaning men. But unfortunately for faith, happiness has not been its fruit. Ireland is full of faith, and full of misery. Also in Spain, Portugal, Italy, and Mexico, faith and bigotry reign triumphant, whilst strife and wretchedness cover those lands.

Wherever superstition has lighted her fire, and put on her seething-pot, the passions of men have boiled over like the lava from Mount Etna, scattering misery, death, and desolation, around. The very names of vice and virtue have been made in many instances to change places. Horrible crimes have been committed under the supposed sanction of a merciful God, while the most sacred duties have been neglected under the apprehension of his displeasure.

The mind becomes confused, distorted, and, not unfrequently, totally subverted by the strong excitements induced by a blind superstitious faith; yet, because excitement is necessary to man, forming as it does a portion of his very being, devotion in one form or another will perhaps always obtain. It may be stripped of blind faith and unmeaning ceremony, it may be rendered comparatively rational and subservient to the growth of human happiness, but it cannot probably be exterminated. Devotion is not so much faith as a feeling of the mind, a deep and intense passion pervading the heart, and mingling with the being of him who has devoted his life to the attainment of a great and good object.

IGNORANCE AND DEVOTION.

The old proverb, "Ignorance is the mother of devotion," is conclusively proven by the well-known fact, that among an ignorant and superstitious people there is little or no free inquiry, doubt, and scepticism. These qualities indicate intelligence, knowledge, progress; and hence it is that we find them prevailing in countries which are the most intellectual, which have made the greatest improvement in the knowledge of themselves and the world they inhabit. Among these nations, England, France, Germany, and America stand preëminent. Accordingly we witness that in these nations the doubts and disbelief of the prevailing system of religion have kept pace with the gradual extension of knowledge. The deep-rooted prejudices of a long succession of ages are daily giving way to the truths of reason and philosophy, and the rays of science are steadily dispelling the mists of superstition.

In the Bible, the standard of their religion, the Christians have long seen something radically defective, or at least not as it should be; but, never once doubting its divine origin, a thought concerning which they have been taught to believe a heinous sin, they have attributed its incomprehensibilities to misinterpretation, and forthwith proceeded to adopt constructions of their own on indistinct and incoherent passages, as if an emanation from the Deity would not have been so plain that he who ran might not only read but comprehend! Hence have arisen the variety of sects in the Christian religion, a variety that is unknown in any other religious system; and a convincing proof to the unprejudiced, that if a perfect Deity found it necessary, after endowing man with the inherent power of distinguishing between good and evil, to furnish him with written instructions, the Bible does not contain them.

CRIME.

The causes and remedy for crime and the moral degradation of the race is an abstruse question, and some superficial remarks or erroneous hypothesis might lead to some correct views on the subject. Without endorsing the doctrine of total depravity, or the other extreme, the perfection of the race, we have no doubt circumstances might or will be attained to modify the organization of man, so that he will exhibit a more rational character. Combe, in his "Constitution of Man," in speaking of witchcraft, says, that Christianity has failed to protect mankind from practical errors; revelation, with all its extra mundane agencies, is a failure.

Hence a sound practical education is the only remedy that the human mind can conceive of to practically protect man from his practical errors; hence his education should commence in forming correct habits in the room of stuffing his mind about phantoms in the dark; his moral sentiments should take the place of his animal sentiments, so that he should have a higher conception of himself than to live for the purpose of gratifying his pride and vanity by dress, ostentation, and parade.

His intellect must be confined to realities, not

the realm of fiction. In fact, it seems that with a correct education, many of the evils of society would vanish. These views may be as inconsistent or Utopian as some others, but they were suggested by comments made upon the increase of crime.

MORALITY.

No man needs a revelation to teach him morality. It grows out of the very nature of man, and is taught him by all his experience and observation from the earliest recollections until his knowledge and judgment are perfectly matured. The principle of it is nowhere to be met with in the Jewish code of laws. It is to be met with in the Christian code, as taught in the New Testament, but there is a great deal also taught there which is inconsistent with it; and therefore, as a whole, the morality of the New Testament is neither pure nor good. We find this principle more fully and more clearly developed in the moral maxims of Confucius; but it is doubted whether this principle *of doing as we would be done by* has ever yet been carried into effect, in practice, to any great extent amongst mankind.

The object of morality is, not only to produce the greatest happiness of the greatest number, but also the greatest happiness of the whole mass, embracing and including all the individuals who compose that mass. Not that all should be equally happy at all times, or even at any time, for this we believe to be absolutely impracticable, if not physically impossible; but only that all should be made as happy at all times as practicable to make them, without encroaching too much on the happiness of others; so that the sacrifice shall in no instance be greater, if so great, as the happiness promoted thereby. To hit upon a plan that will best effect this, will probably require many experiments; for we do not believe that the best experiment has ever yet been tried.

THIS WORLD.

One world at a time is quite enough to attend to, nor does there seem to be any good reason for attending to another, since it must be self-evident that when mankind know how to live properly on the earth, they are prepared to live in heaven, if there be any such place in reserve for them. But without this indispensable preparation, it will not be a very desirable residence, even when they arrive there, and hence we may say, that whether in regard to this world or another, our Infidel doctrine is the only proper one for either.

It is true that men are seldom so absorbed in thoughts of heaven as to be without care or interest for the good things of earth, and that if the first day of the week belong to God, the other six are considered as belonging to Mammon. But this only proves that men are as inconsistent in following out their principles, as they are irrational in adopting them. If heaven be a reality, as we are told it is, it *ought* to absorb our thoughts, and to constitute the sole end and aim of our actions.

We shall perhaps be told, that man would faint and sink under temporal afflictions, but for the consolations derived from heavenly or spiritual hopes. We admit that anticipations of a heaven of bliss excite and give pleasure for the moment. Perhaps the opium-eater, in his ecstatic reveries, was never more perfectly blessed than some enthusiasts have been in their dreams of paradise. But opium, though it offers a seducing mode of escaping from present pain, is yet exceedingly pernicious in its after effects. Depression succeeds to unnatural excitement, and moments of bliss are followed by days of misery. Visions of another world seem to us to act as a sort of moral opium, often no less injurious to the Christian than his favorite solace is to the Turk.

But men must be wretched indeed, if to save themselves from despair, they must resort to artificial stimuli, physical or moral; and we believe that in every case the remedy is worse than the disease. Nay, more; the remedy *perpetuates* the disease. If a man, to escape his cares, resorts to the bottle, his cares will soon increase and ruin him. And if, to quiet the anxieties of life, we have recourse to the excitements of religion, shall we not be similarly situated? Let us hope for the time when knowledge shall dispel the worst miseries of life.

www.ingramcontent.com/pod-product-compliance
Lightning Source LLC
Chambersburg PA
CBHW021824230426
43669CB00008B/855